"In this book my pastor and ————————— in
my life. Knowing the one per——— of
the only true hope in bringing c———— :e
it is inevitable that we will all dea——— s
to rest secure in the hope we have———— s
us unpack."

Von.   ..,gnt, co-founder, Campus Crusade
for Christ International/Cru

"In *Everlasting Life*, David Swanson has not only faithfully addressed the core fear we all share—the fear of death—he has thrown open the curtains on the great hope that is ours through the work of Jesus. Indeed, the gospel doesn't just prepare us to die; it equips us to live. With personal anecdotes, great theology, and an engaged heart, David helps us see that the abundant and everlasting life Jesus offers us is so much better than we could have ever hoped or imagined. This book will encourage the hearts of many, believers and nonbelievers alike."

Scotty Smith, pastor and author of *Everyday Prayers*

"*Everlasting Life* tackles the challenging subjects of facing death, the spiritual process of dying, and what the glorious but mysterious afterlife of heaven might be like from a biblical perspective. Scripture is used well and explained with understandable examples that will undoubtedly stick with the reader to create a lasting and comforting impact. This book will educate and enlarge the reader's perspective on Christianly facing the end of one's life or comforting someone else at that juncture so as to assist in alleviating anxieties and concerns about the transition from this life to the next. The reader is helped to develop a happy and eager anticipation of what is in store for all of us if we accept Christ in our hearts."

Bob DeVries and Susan Zonnebelt-Smeenge,
authors of *Getting to the Other Side of Grief*

"*Everlasting Life* presents strong biblical truth expressed with wisdom and gentleness. Pastor David Swanson offers comfort to the grieving, gives insight to the comforter, and shares the gospel with those who do not yet believe in Christ. He helps the reader face the fact of his or her own death and addresses why death is in the world. Through a series of questions he confronts our fears of death. I value his emphasis on the significance of the body and his granting those who mourn permission to grieve. His personal illustrations are compelling, showing that his words are rooted in experience. *Everlasting Life* is more than a primer on grief. it is a theology of death, of life, and of the life to come. It is balm for a broken heart and fuel for good pastoral care."

David Wiersbe, author of *Gone but Not Lost*

"This is a book that every Christian needs to read as part of their disciple-ship. We all need this primer on dying, death, grief, and our eternal hope. I would urge pastors, deacons, spouses, parents, and adult children, plus all good friends, to read this for those days when we have the privilege of walking with someone through the valley of the shadow of death. And all of us will—for this is a subject we all need to know."

Jim Singleton, associate professor of pastoral leadership
and evangelism, Gordon-Conwell Theological Seminary

"I have had the privilege of knowing David for seven years. Everyone who knows him knows that he has a heart for God, and that love is transferred into everyone he meets. With this book David uses his God-given talent and personal experiences to reach a multitude of people. He clearly provides us with knowledge, peace, and hope, using the truth of God's Word, as we experience the transformation from everyday life to eternal life in heaven. The details he supplies of the dos and don'ts of what to say and what to do for the dying, at funerals, and for those left behind are immeasurably important aspects that we should practice. I highly recommend this book, which will encourage you and help you as you interact with the real-life issues that you face."

Dr. David Uth, senior pastor, First Baptist Orlando

"Death is the great equalizer. No one escapes. But there is life beyond death, as David Swanson explains. Refreshingly personal and practical, this is a book you will want to read and then share with those who are facing loss, grieving, and searching for hope."

Luder Whitlock, president emeritus, Reformed Theological Seminary

"I conducted seven funerals in the eighteen days before I read *Everlasting Life* by David Swanson. These memorial services were for people I had known and loved, some for as long as thirty-five years. When I sat down with this book in my lap, I was weary. After forty-seven years in pastoral ministry, I know the physical, emotional, and spiritual fatigue that accompanies grief.

"As I read *Everlasting Life*, I found comfort and refreshment. The book is biblically based and theologically sound. More than that, it is written as a first-person account from the heart of a loving pastor. Swanson invites us on a three-part journey down a well-traveled path. That pilgrimage begins with facing death as a reality for all of us. We walk on holy ground as we confront the great mystery of our mortality. Finally, we make the transition to the life beyond.

"The afternoon after I finished reading *Everlasting Life*, I visited the grave of our son. Erik died when he was twenty-seven years old. I thought of his journey and of mine. David of Bethlehem described it as a trek through the dark valley of the shadow, where we need fear no evil because our Shepherd is with us. David of Orlando follows that tradition, encouraging us to enter that brave and glorious venture.

"If you are grieving, read *Everlasting Life*. If you know someone who is bereaved, share the book with them. It will minister to others as it has to me."

Kirk H. Neely, senior pastor and author, *When Grief Comes*

Everlasting **Life**

How God Answers Our Questions about
Grief, Loss, and the Promise of Heaven

David D. SWANSON

BakerBooks

a division of Baker Publishing Group
Grand Rapids, Michigan

© 2013 by David D. Swanson

Published by Baker Books
a division of Baker Publishing Group
P.O. Box 6287, Grand Rapids, MI 49516-6287
www.bakerbooks.com

Printed in the United States of America

Library of Congress Cataloging-in-Publication Data is on file at the Library of Congress, Washington, DC.

ISBN 978-0-8010-1446-8

13   14   15   16   17   18   19   7   6   5   4   3   2   1

Dedication

To my mother, Nancy Swanson, who faithfully endured the loss of her father on Christmas Day, 1957, and who encouraged my yearning for heaven through the manner in which she grieved in the hope of Christ.

In Memoriam

In their living and dying, God used the lives of these faithful people to shape my understanding of his faithfulness in this life—and the next.

Delmar and Sabina Mock	Barrett Burchak
Don and Viola Swanson	Frank Lindrum
Dorothy Cooper	Bob Hewitt
Dick Bywaters	Ruff Robinson
Mallory Blake	Lane Newsom Drennan
Calvin Baird	Fred Ryan

Contents

Contents

Foreword

Two statements in Scripture stand like the north and south poles of the vast mystery that is our nature. One comes from the prophet Isaiah: "All flesh is as the grass" (Isa. 40:6 NKJV). We are that way. The grass is here today and gone tomorrow. That is the way of all things earthly: the trees that outlast us and the flowers that are outlasted by us; the pets we nurture; the people whom we brush up against each day; our parents and children and spouses. From early on, when the hints of mortality begin to make our skin sag and our muscles ache, we know it is true. All flesh is as the grass.

The other statement is also ancient, from the Teacher in Ecclesiastes: "He [God] has also set eternity in the human heart" (Eccl. 3:11). We may be mortal as the grass, but inside is a longing that the mere recitation of the immutable laws of nature cannot still. As a friend of mine says, we want *more*. No matter how good our lives or beautiful the earth or long our years or happy our families—we want more.

Death is both the inevitable ending of our existence and the hint that *more* has not yet played out. We fear it, hide from it, ignore it, and pretend that our technology can overcome it, yet there it stands. We have a thousand nicknames for the Grim Reaper, but none say it better than the apostle Paul: death is our enemy (1 Cor. 15:26).

And yet it is to be overcome. And yet it *has been* overcome.

David Swanson speaks with wisdom, grace, and honesty about the ultimate subject of existence. It is a matter he has thought much about; I remember him saying once that a salesman had described him as someone who has already bought his last mattress. (I'm not sure people who are not on their last mattress should be allowed to write about death anyway.)

There is much to help you in these pages. There is good theology. There is sage guidance on how to be with people who suffer from illness, people who fear death, people who have lost someone they love.

But most of all, there is *hope*. It is not a vague hope, not an elusive shot in the dark. Here you will discover a hope beyond optimism, a hope beyond doctors' diagnoses, a hope built on the one man who has looked death square in the eye. Jesus went into the tomb and came out the other side and told us that death is not the end, that all flesh may be as grass but eternity is already in session.

So read on, about life and death and life beyond death.

Read on and hope.

John Ortberg

Acknowledgments

God's timing is always perfect. I know that and I trust that, but I don't always understand it. When I first agreed to write this book, I had no idea what events would unfold as I did the actual work of writing it. Without question, the past eighteen months have been the most challenging in my twenty-one years of ministry, made all the more so by trying to write a book on grief, death, and heaven in the midst of the challenges. On more than one occasion, feeling battered by events, I sat down to write without much energy or interest in doing so, only to have the Holy Spirit meet me in that place and minister to my soul as I reflected on God's promises about this world—and the next. While I felt the burden of having to meet deadlines for my writing, I discovered that God was actually ministering to me in the process. Writing this book became a lifeline—a touchstone—in the midst of all that was happening around me.

First Presbyterian Church, Orlando, which I am privileged to pastor, went through the long and arduous process of being dismissed from the Presbyterian Church (USA) so that we could join the Evangelical Presbyterian Church. It was an experience that I would not trade, but it is not one that I want to go through again. God was faithful to us in so many ways, and our body inspired me daily as I watched their consistent, unwavering witness to the lordship of Jesus Christ and the authority of God's Word. There were two Sundays during the process when God's Spirit arrived in a way that I had never known, and I attribute that to the faithful prayers of this great congregation. God honored their courage even as they sought to honor him.

Through the process there were many people who took on significant roles, people who removed enormous burdens from my shoulders, creating enough space for me to actually serve and minister—and write. Dianna Morgan, one of our elders, was indispensable. Her humble, wise, and faithful manner reflected her deep love for God and her service to this church, and she honored the Lord beautifully. Sam Knight, an associate pastor at the time and now interim senior pastor at Grace Presbyterian Church in Houston, Texas, served with unflagging energy and commitment. His knowledge of polity and governance, as well as his poised demeanor, facilitated our process beyond anything I could have done.

Our Task Force on Dismissal, a committee of our Session charged with shepherding our body through the process of dismissal, served Christ beautifully. We met together more times than any of us care to remember, but I am deeply indebted to each of them: Christy Wilson, Kevin Taylor, Erica Saunders, and Craig Clayton. In addition to those four, Greg McNeill joined us toward the end and provided focused legal counsel. Greg is a dear friend and regular golf companion, but more importantly, he is one of the smartest people I know, always calm and steady in the storm. His efforts on behalf of our Session and congregation were tremendous gifts for which I will always be indebted.

My senior leadership team at First Presbyterian Church were wonderful, caring colleagues as well. Without their constant presence and gifted ministry, I would not have been able to survive. Along with Sam Knight, they are Rebecca Bedell, Donna McClellan, Case Thorp, and John Watts.

My assistant, Grace Whitlow, was also an enormous part of this process as she kept my office humming peacefully even in the face of so many issues and needs. Her unflappable, calm nature was something I marveled at often, and she helped keep me calm even as things appeared to be spinning wildly. What a gift she is to me and to our church.

My secret editor on this project was Paula Lindrum, who also serves as my assistant for The Well, my online media ministry (www.drinkfromthewell.com). As one who was walking freshly in her own grief following the death of her husband, Frank, she was the first one to read each completed chapter. Her insightful, Spirit-led comments helped bring clarity to many ideas and concepts, and her eye for grammar and misspelled words proved a necessary gift.

Finally, I owe much to my wife, Leigh. She read every chapter and honestly shared her thoughts and feelings. She loves me enough to gently tell me the truth—an art often lost in our culture today. Through it all, she loved me—unconditionally, freely, tenderly, graciously she loved me. She is the joy in my journey.

And my children, John David, Alex, and Kaylee, are God's great gifts to me. No matter the stress I was facing or the issues gnawing at my heart, the pure joy of being their father always brought me needed perspective, laughter, hope, escape, and sheer delight. I love you and thank you for enriching my life beyond measure.

Introduction

That life only really begins when it ends here on earth, that all that is here is only the prologue before the curtain goes up—that is for young and old alike to think about.

Dietrich Bonhoeffer

When the perishable has been clothed with the imperishable, and the mortal with immortality, then the saying that is written will come true: "Death has been swallowed up in victory."

1 Corinthians 15:54

Sitting in a waiting room was about the last thing I wanted to be doing at that moment. For heaven's sake, it was the middle of summer and I hadn't had any time off since Christmas. I was tired and cranky and ready for some relaxation, but there I was nonetheless.

My wife and I had flown with our three children to Dallas where most of our extended family lives, including my oldest sister, Susan, a physician in that area. Susan is a wonderful person who has a persistent way of keeping an eye on my personal health. Knowing

15

I have a rather high-stress job and that I was approaching fifty, she insisted that while we were in Dallas I go see a friend of hers for a complete *executive* physical. I didn't want to be there but knew I needed to be.

That morning I discovered she had not signed me up for your average run-of-the-mill physical. Oh no, this thing lasted six hours. I had every test you can imagine. By the time I finished, I felt like a human pincushion. I had a treadmill stress test. I had blood drawn. I had a body fat analysis. I had a CT scan of my lungs. I had pictures taken of my throat and vocal chords. I had an echocardiogram of my heart. I filled out a forty-page questionnaire about my physical exercise and dietary routines as well as questions about my mental and emotional health. To say that it was a thorough exam would be the understatement of the decade.

When I finally finished, I met with the doctor for thirty minutes to go over the preliminary findings, and while he indicated I was in reasonably good shape, his comments were hardly unequivocal. He told me that after a few more test results came in, he would mail me a detailed report, including recommendations I would need to follow to maximize my personal health.

Sure enough, three weeks later the packet arrived. I opened it, expecting to find a letter that said something to the effect of, "Dr. Swanson, after an extensive review of all your tests, I am thoroughly impressed by your good health and find that you have the physical stature of a man half your age. Well done!" Instead, the letter informed me that while I was in reasonably good health, there were twelve things—*twelve*—I needed to focus on if I wanted to improve my health and eliminate some potential risk factors for future disease.

I was stunned. I knew my diet was not as healthy as it should be. I knew I needed to watch my sugar intake and exercise more, but for crying out loud, come on—*twelve things*—really? As I sat there scanning the exhaustive list, I realized I had a choice to make. The doctor was essentially telling me that if I wanted to live for as long as possible—if I wanted to do all I could to fend off death until the last possible moment—then I needed to change some of my behavior patterns. The question was obvious: Was I willing to make those changes? Was I willing to change my behavior to live as long as I possibly could?

As I contemplated what I was willing and not willing to do, I started thinking about the notion of eternal life. As a Christian, I believe in heaven, the afterlife, and immortality. And that's when it all hit me right between the eyes: How should my behavior change in light of the fact that I will *never* die? Gulp. I know it sounds like I've lost my mind, but think about it. If you believe what the Bible says about eternity and heaven, then physically we may die, but spiritually we never die. The essence of who we are goes on, albeit in a different form. So if that's true, and I stake my life on it, then the question becomes: How should my view, my perspective, of life in this world change in light of my faith in Christ, which tells me I am going to live forever?

The question rattled me. Yes, I needed to work on changing some of my personal habits for better physical health, but I was gripped by a totally different reality: through our faith in Christ, we are actually *immortal*. Wrap your brain around that for a second. Our being, as created by God, never dies. This is not a pleasant-sounding myth or manmade psychological crutch; it is a promised reality. Scripture reminds us of this over and over again. In Christ, *we are immortal* "through the appearing of our Savior, Christ Jesus, who has destroyed death and has brought life and immortality to light through the gospel" (2 Tim. 1:10). That's not a reference to the immortality of Christ, but instead it is the declaration of *our* immortality through the gospel of Jesus Christ. What is the gospel? It is the Good News of God revealed in Christ, the Good News that Christ has opened the door to our salvation by his death and resurrection.

Perhaps more famously, Paul, while discussing the absolute certainty of the resurrection, writes in 1 Corinthians 15:52–54:

> In a flash, in the twinkling of an eye, at the last trumpet. . . . The trumpet will sound, the dead will be raised imperishable, and we will be changed. For the perishable must clothe itself with the

imperishable, and the mortal with immortality. When the perishable has been clothed with the imperishable, and the mortal with immortality, then the saying that is written will come true: "Death has been swallowed up in victory."

Paul declares that there will be a day when our greatest enemy, death, will be swallowed up in the victory of Jesus, and we will be immortal. We will enter into the glorious hope of our everlasting life. Our being, as God made us, never dies. If we are in Christ, we live forever. It may well be the most hope-inducing truth in all of Scripture, given our fear of death. It is the hope of everlasting life.

As you try to grasp the magnitude of that, let me ask you a question: If this is true, then shouldn't that also shape an enormous part of how we think and behave in this life? Shouldn't it give us a completely different lens through which we view life on this planet? Think about it. Our culture today invests enormous resources, not to mention huge amounts of time and energy, in health care, medicine, and fitness. It's almost impossible *not* to think about our physical health and all that we need to do to prolong our earthly life. But comparatively, do we spend any time considering the alternate reality that we will never die spiritually?

At the core of our investment in health and fitness is our deep desire to fend off physical death. Yet at some point we must acknowledge we will never succeed. Eventually our number comes up. Therefore, if we are going to be spiritually and emotionally healthy people, we need to consider what happens beyond this life. We need to spend some time wrestling with those questions instead of just the questions motivated by our physical existence. We need to face the prospect of our demise and all that is associated with it; thus, my purpose in this book is to help you do just that. I want to help you bring the subject to the surface and walk around it, see it, touch it, and feel it, and in so doing, grow comfortable in the truths that God has revealed about our physical lives and our spiritual immortality through Christ. I believe those truths can have life-changing consequences for both this life and the next.

Acknowledging the Inevitable

In spite of the cultural emphasis on this physical life, the specter of our death and what may lie beyond it is always there. Sometimes quiet, sometimes roaring, sometimes lurking just beyond the grasp of conscious thought—death waits.

Still, most people do everything they can to avoid it. In my twenty-three years as a pastor, I have spent innumerable days immersed in matters of life and death. I have prayed at the beds of the dying, held the hands of family members as they coped with crushing loss, visited funeral homes with grieving spouses to help them pick out caskets and burial plots, anointed foreheads, wiped tears, written eulogies, and watched many take their last breath. Even so, as I move and minister among my congregation and in our community, I find this odd reluctance to talk about death and dying, at least among those not readily facing it. When's the last time you were at a social gathering and heard someone say, "Well, I've really been giving some thought to the end of my life, and here's what I think . . ."? It just never happens, does it?

At times, however, we do hear people at social gatherings muster the courage to share a recent loss. Someone will say, "Yeah, I've been out of town for a few weeks taking care of my mother. She finally died last Tuesday." In spite of the enormous vulnerability that person most surely feels, what happens? Eyes immediately drop to the floor. No one quite knows what to do next. "I'm so sorry," we say. Uncomfortable shuffling of feet follows. All involved are trying to think of a deft way to change the subject. It's awkward because no one wants to go there. It puts a huge damper on the conversation. The subject of death is a big wet blanket, smothering people with feelings and thoughts they would much rather avoid. We are more comfortable keeping death in the shadows. I'm not saying that's right or wrong. It's value-neutral. I think it's just a very basic part of our human nature.

Several years ago, John Cloud, a senior writer for *Time* magazine, wrote a marvelous piece for that publication entitled "A Kinder, Gentler Death." It appeared on the cover with the subhead,

"Dying on Our Own Terms." It was a poignant examination of end-of-life issues in which he wrote:

> Dying is one of the few events certain to occur in life and yet Americans as a whole have a hard time discussing it. Although many Americans legally designate someone else to make medical decisions after they are unable to, 30 percent of those designated do not know they have been picked.[1]

That statistic doesn't surprise me. They don't know they were designated because so many people don't want to bring up the subject. Most of us want to avoid it as much as we can, mainly because we view it as a one-dimensional conversation that's always about death, never about life, and that always contains seemingly unanswerable questions. Because we are not acquainted with the God-given answers available to us in Scripture, we don't want to bring up the questions. And if, by chance, the question does sneak into a conversation, we'll throw out a perfunctory comment and change the subject as quickly as we can, retreating into our psychological defenses that remind us, *I'm healthy. That's not going to happen to me, at least not for a long time.*

Another of our favorite defense mechanisms is to mock death, as though somehow by thumbing our nose at it, we can prevent it from touching us. I remember reading about an annual celebration in a tiny mountain community in Colorado that really caught me off guard. Since 2001 the town of Nederland has hosted Frozen Dead Guy Days. I know. Seems strange to me too, but I am not making this up. It started when Grandpa Bredo Morstoel died in 1989 in Norway, and a family member, hoping to start her own cryogenics business, brought his frozen body to Nederland, Colorado. When local authorities found out about it, the practice of storing bodies was outlawed, but Mr. Morstoel was grandfathered in and allowed to stay in town. The town, seeing its opportunity to laugh in the face of death, started the festival. There was a frozen dead guy in their town, so why not?

Today 20,000 people attend. There are coffin races and lots of beer, and for a mere $150 you get a personal visit to the remains of

Mr. Morstoel. Festival director Amanda MacDonald says the goal is "to drink a convivial toast to the grim specter of death or to spit in death's eye."[2] This gleefully macabre weekend built around a frozen corpse—a frozen dead guy!—is yet another example of how we finite human beings try to cope with our pending physical demise.

Why do we avoid and mock death? Aside from the obvious reasons, I think its mystery is a large factor. I love it when the apostle Paul, beginning a discourse on our immortality, says, "Listen, I tell you a mystery" (1 Cor. 15:51). Before he launches into some of the specifics of what God wants to reveal about our journey from this life to the next, he says, "Hey, pay attention! Listen up! I am going to tell you some things about death and dying and the life that is to come. But the first point I need to make is this: it's a *mystery*. You will never, in your finite minds, grasp this fully."

Death is the great and vast unknown, and like it or not, things that are deeply mysterious or beyond our mental reach usually frighten us. Statistics from a 2003 national survey show that while 92 percent of Americans believe in God and 85 percent believe in heaven, their beliefs bring them little solace in regard to their fear of death.[3] The hope of our faith in Christ is somehow not getting through. Thus, in our fear, we deny its reality.

Finding the Answers to the Mystery

Like most mysteries, death leaves us asking questions. While we'd like to figure it out, it is so unpleasant to us that we don't make any real effort to find answers. As I said, we avoid it, at least until we realize it's not going away. While this realization comes on us at different times and in different ways, at some point it does come. Anna Quindlen says death becomes "an enduring thing called loss."[4] We do not get over it. The actual death may pass, but then we are left with something larger— an abyss called *loss* that endures. Emily Dickinson described our dance with death as "an awful leisure."[5] It is awful, and it seems to be in no hurry. Death lingers in an almost leisurely way in spite of our best efforts

21

to elude it. Thus, if death endures and lingers long, then the only way we can hope to ever find relief from our fears and anxieties on this subject is to find answers. If it's not going away, then we need to find hope. Well, here's the good news: God *does* provide answers. God is not going to tell us everything, but he does give us insights and glimpses into the mystery of death such that we can find peace and security.

Here's the thing: when we have questions in this life and we go to God, God *wants* to answer. He delights in revealing himself to us. Throughout the Scriptures, God is not trying to remain hidden. He wants to be known.[6] That is most clearly seen in the incarnation of Jesus Christ. If God did not want to be known, then Jesus would never have come. God further affirms in Matthew 7:8, "The one who seeks finds." God tells us in James 1:5, "If any of you lacks wisdom, you should ask God, who gives generously." If we feel we lack understanding on something, God says *ask*. He's not trying to keep us in the dark, and my hope is that in this book you will discover the wonder of how God answers most of our questions on death and dying through himself. Ultimately, *God* is the answer.

This is never more evident than in the moments when Jesus faced death. In that awful, horrific scene, Matthew 27:46 reminds us that Jesus asked a question. It was not a question rising out of some gentle curiosity. It was a question that welled up from a place deep within him—a question that was literally shouted from the depths of his being. Jesus cried out in a loud voice, "My God, my God, why have you forsaken me?" As piercing as that moment is for us to consider, it should also bring us great freedom and confidence.

If as Jesus faced death and all its mysteries, he asked God a question, then we have been set free to do so as well. And we have been set free to ask God with all the emotion and earnestness that we may be feeling at any given time. We don't have to whimper the questions. If we are hurting and lost, we can cry out to the living God, and he promises to hear us—and to bring us his presence. In the agony of death, Jesus turned to the Father for answers and relief, and that should be our plan too. Answers to these questions are found nowhere else.

We should also remember that two others died along with Jesus that day, and one of them asked a question of Jesus. In Luke 23:39, one of the thieves asked, "Aren't you the Messiah? Save yourself and us!" I think it was mainly a rhetorical question, a command of sorts more than an honest question. The thief was essentially asking, "If you are God, then get me down from here and I'll believe you!" The thief wanted Jesus to get him out of his current situation. But before Jesus could respond to the first thief, the second thief asked the first thief a question: "Don't you fear God . . . since you are under the same sentence?" (Luke 23:40). The second thief seemed to suggest that, given his position, the first thief should probably not be making any demands. Then the second thief said to Jesus, "Remember me when you come into your kingdom" (Luke 23:42).

The beauty of their exchange is this: while the first thief wanted Jesus in order to change his circumstances, the second thief accepted his circumstances—and death—as long as he could be with Jesus. As he was dying, the second thief realized that all his questions about the moment of his passing were held in the life of one man: Jesus Christ. He didn't ask to get out of his circumstances; he just asked for Jesus. Therefore, like that second thief, we also come to Jesus. We come to him not so he can get us out of the physical reality of death, but rather so we can find the answers to our fears—and the hope of everlasting life—in *him*.

Shining Light on Death

I keep a flashlight by my bed. It's one of those enormous Maglite flashlights that you can also use as a weapon if needed—but it's mainly there for the light. Why? At times, the darkness scares me. I don't know what's there; however, if I light it up with my flashlight, it's suddenly much less frightening. I can see what's there. My fears abate.

The same is true in our dance with death. If death is an inevitable part of our life that seems to linger in the shadows, then we need to confront and shine the light of life on it. Avoiding it or denying its reality leaves us in an unhealthy, fearful darkness that, if allowed to persist, can have negative consequences.

If we don't confront our fears and seek answers to our questions, we will live more to avoid death instead of embracing life. We will obsess over the health or activity of our loved ones. We will start to limit our own activities, whether consciously or unconsciously. No airplanes or white-water rafting. No mission trips to foreign countries. No unnecessary risks. We live as though we have to protect our life instead of living our life to the full as Jesus intended (John 10:10). What we need is some light, and that light is found in Jesus. Thus, you can think of this book as a big flashlight!

Over the course of my life and ministry, here's what I've found: while people may not want to talk about the shadowy mystery of death, *they know they need to.* They may feel uncomfortable, but at some level they recognize death's inevitability and the need to talk about it in some way. We need to shine God's light on death. We need to start to see death for what it is and begin to place it in its proper context. This is where a broader perspective becomes so important. Our reluctance to talk about death, with all its fears and anxieties, would be tempered if our perspective were not so limited by the things of this world. We think and act and respond based solely on our existence in this life. If just for a moment we could take our eyes off what is here and catch a glimpse of what is to come, wouldn't that perspective change how we view all that we endure on this planet?

Several years ago I announced to the congregation of First Presbyterian Church, Orlando, that I would be preaching a series on death and dying. Many thought I was trying to kill attendance (insert laugh track here). In all seriousness, the Discussing the Inevitable series became the most requested, most downloaded, most purchased sermon series I have ever preached. The overwhelming response reinforced what I already knew: people don't want to talk about it, but they know they need to. They need a grid—a framework—for making sense of this looming specter, and that grid must include the entire journey. For the Christian, death is the shortest part of that journey, and if we are ever to learn to cope with physical loss, we need to grasp the larger reality of our journey toward immortality.

When we understand that, our perspective of death and dying becomes wholly different. That's what I mean when I say we need a new *grid* through which to see this. When we shine God's light on death, the promise of our everlasting life becomes a wonderfully transforming truth. Though death is definitely a mystery, not only do we need to bring up the subject, but we also need the tools to understand what God has revealed in his Word.

A Three-Part Journey

I will spend the rest of this book examining the three elements of our journey from this life to the next, so let me briefly introduce you to each element as we find them revealed in 1 Corinthians 15.

Part 1: Up Close and Personal with Death

The first part of our journey is the physical life we live now. In verse 39 Paul gives us a very *fleshy* review of how we have been made: "Not all flesh is the same: People have one kind of flesh, animals have another, birds another and fish another." He then goes on to say that these physical bodies are not permanent but perishable. He writes beginning in verses 42–44, "The body that is sown is perishable, it is raised imperishable; it is sown in dishonor, it is raised in glory; it is sown in weakness, it is raised in power; it is sown a natural body, it is raised a spiritual body."

During this part of the journey, we live a life that is perishable, described by Paul with two key words: *dishonor* and *weakness*. God has made it clear that we live in a fallen world marked by sin and death. Even those who love God deeply and follow him obediently are bound by this world's dishonor and weakness. I am reminded of a translation of Aeschylus, quoted by Robert F. Kennedy in his speech announcing Martin Luther King Jr.'s assassination on April 4, 1968:

25

Even in our sleep, pain which cannot forget
falls drop by drop upon the heart
until, in our own despair, against our will,
comes wisdom through the awful grace of God.[7]

It is the nature of this life, and we must acknowledge its dishonor and pain, an acknowledgment that only serves to deepen our hunger for the life to come.

Part 2: From Here to There

The second leg of our journey is marked by movement, and this is where we enter into some of the more profound mysteries. Paul uses a series of words (1 Cor. 15:42, 53) that describe our movement from this life to the next:

from perishable to imperishable

from dishonor to glory

from weakness to power

from natural to spiritual

from mortal to immortality

Paul says that we are clearly moving from one life to the next, taking a journey from one form of existence into another. Jesus describes this movement in John 14:3, "I will come back and take you to be with me that you also may be where I am."

In the mystery of God, I'll be the first to say I'm not totally sure how it all works. But from Scripture I do know that Jesus is the one who takes us on the journey. He is the one who helps us move from this life into the next.

In the spiritual realm, we depart this life and Jesus takes us to be with him where he lives. What joy there must be when we begin that second part of our journey! For that reason, the words of John Donne can ring true in our hearts:

Death be not proud, though some have called thee
Mighty and dreadfull, for, thou art not so.[8]

We fear death, calling it mighty and proud, but it is not. By faith in Christ, physical death is only the end of the first part of our journey. The second part moves us out of the realm of death and into the realm of life, all in the arms of Jesus. So death, be not proud, for we are going home!

Part 3: Everlasting Life

The third and final part of this journey is when we come to our heart's true home, our eternal dwelling place in the heavenly realms of God. This journey is captured in the powerful words of Paul:

> Listen, I tell you a mystery: We will not all sleep, but we will all be changed—in a flash, in the twinkling of an eye. . . . For the perishable must clothe itself with the imperishable, and the mortal with immortality, . . . then the saying that is written will come true: "Death has been swallowed up in victory."
>
> 1 Corinthians 15:51–54

Recently, Billy Graham released what will most likely be his final book. *Nearing Home: Life, Faith, and Finishing Well* is filled with his reflections on his failing physical strength, his anticipation of what is to come, and the importance of bearing witness to Christ even in one's final days.[9] Because of the stature of his life and the way he has lived it, Dr. Graham's reflections on his final days will no doubt draw others to consider how they are living as well. That kind of reflection always seems to happen to people at funerals or memorial services. The setting makes them contemplate their own lives. They usually hear about how someone lived and feel compelled to examine their own life by comparison.

Not long ago, one of the patriarchs of our church died after a long illness. Two days after the funeral, one of his sons came to my office and talked about his father's legacy, saying he wanted to grow to be the kind of leader and the kind of servant his father was. Taking in the fact that his father's life had ended produced an internal wrestling, a time of deep personal reflection for that young man. I am confident that his reflections on his father's death will yield fruit for God's kingdom, both in the present and in the future. It is that kind of personal reflection we all need to engage in before we wind up sitting in a memorial service. Why wait until then to ask the questions and find the hope?

Yes, we need to talk about life lessons and the things of this world. But we also need moments and opportunities, like funerals or books or the beauty of deep personal conversation with a friend, to lead us into a richer exploration of this final part of our journey.

That said, if you picked up this book thinking it was going to answer every question about death or what happens in the next life, you will be sorely disappointed. We are never going to know everything there is to know about this life or the next, about living or dying, about what we do in the next life or how we leave this one. There is too much mystery in it. God has not given us all the details, but he has given us the truth of his Word, and by examining it closely, we find a new perspective that brings security and hope.

I don't know about you, but that is perspective I need. I am emboldened and encouraged in this life when I realize—and internalize—that nothing in this life can defeat me. Not death. Not illness. Not grief. Not addiction. Not miscarriages and infertility. Not financial losses. Not unemployment. *Nothing* can defeat me. We celebrate what John declares in Revelation 21:4, "He will wipe every tear from their eyes. There will be no more death or mourning or crying or pain, for the old order of things has passed away." That's our future home. That's our final destination.

Homesick

Over the past twenty-three years of ministry, God has put me in some very challenging places where lives have been tragically lost. Often, when these families have emerged from those depths, they will say something to me that generally goes like this: "I don't see how you do this all the time. You were with us when we went through one of the lowest points in our life, but once you finished with us, you had to deal with another family coping with another loss. How do you survive all that and still maintain some sense of joy in life?"

My answer to that is this book. I have certainly had to learn the art of temporarily insulating myself from deep emotions in order to minister to those who grieve. I have been through a number of funerals where I have worked my way through the entire service and the reception and then stepped into my office, sat down, and sobbed. I am no spiritual giant or superman.

Even through my tears, however, I move forward in the joy and peace of Christ because of the truth God has revealed. This life is temporary. It's one part of our journey, but it's not the only part, and it's not even the most significant or longest part. It just happens to be the part we're in now.

Dietrich Bonhoeffer wrote, "No one has yet believed in God and the kingdom of God, no one has yet heard about the realm of the resurrected, and not been homesick from that hour, waiting and looking forward joyfully to being released from bodily existence."[10] I like his observation. In the end, I think I'm just homesick. We all are. We want to be set free from the bonds of this life to be reunited with the Father. And we will be. That day *will* come. Our journey goes on from here. When you understand your journey into everlasting life more deeply and more personally, you will not look at this life—with its losses, pains, and heartaches—in the same way again.

I'll spend the rest of this book illuminating our journey toward that life and immortality in the hope that fully grasping the truth that we will never die will change our behavior and our perspective in this life, transforming us by the peace and joy of our eternal life in Jesus Christ.

PART 1

The Journey
Begins

Up Close and Personal
with Our Last Enemy

1

What's Going On Here?

Coming Face-to-Face with Our Old Foe

The sting of death is sin.

1 Corinthians 15:56

I have a deep sense that if we could really befriend death we would be free people. Many people never seem to befriend death and die as if they were losing a hopeless battle. But we do not have to share that sad fate.

Henri J. M. Nouwen, *A Letter of Consolation*

Every single thing about it was wrong. It looked wrong. It smelled wrong. Physically and emotionally, it felt wrong. There was nothing right about it.

I was in my second week as a chaplain intern at a hospital in Austin, Texas, and during my first all-night shift I got my first "death call." My pager went off, flashing the room number. I hurried upstairs. When I entered, the family was present, but the patient was dead. I had never seen a deceased person before, and the sight so shocked me that I found it very difficult to collect my thoughts. I realized very quickly I was of no use to the family and left the room as soon as I could. Embarrassed, I discussed it with my supervisor the next morning. She assured me my reaction was completely natural and that she would help me try to process my thoughts and feelings over the next few days. She told me to take my time, slow down, and not try to process it all at once.

Later that afternoon she came to find me while I was making my rounds and asked me to come with her so I could take a look at something. We went up two flights of stairs and down a long hall of patient rooms until we came to one in particular. She pushed the door open and there in the bed was a deceased woman. She was in her late fifties or perhaps early sixties. She had short salt-and-pepper hair with barrettes holding back one side. Her eyes were mostly closed, her head was tipped back at an angle, and her mouth was wide open, almost as if she was trying to inhale one last breath. In case you didn't know, newly deceased people do not look like they do in funeral homes. Funeral homes try to make a dead person appear as much like a living person as they can. In hospitals, dead people are just dead.

My supervisor went over to the body and put her hand on the woman's arm. She began to describe what a body goes through at the time of death, what some of the possible reactions may be, and through her words, tried to disarm what was so foreign to me. At that point, I was still barely inside the doorway, staring. I felt myself beginning to sweat, and in spite of her calm demeanor, I immediately wanted to leave the room. Seeing my discomfort, she invited me to come closer: "Come here and stand next to the bed with me." Not one part of me wanted to do that, but I knew I needed to. I knew I needed to go over to this cold, deceased body that represented to me all the things I did not want to think about, and I needed to make peace with it. I needed to walk around it and look at it. I needed to linger there with myself and all those feelings, or I would be of no use to anyone as a chaplain in that hospital.

So I did. I walked over, and I looked. My supervisor took the woman's hand on the other side of the bed and said, "Take her hand, like this. It's okay. You can touch her." That next moment may have been one of the most meaningful and yet frightening moments of my life. I picked up and held the hand of a dead woman. It was cold, almost the way a piece of wet clay feels. And stiff. It did not move like a living hand. Part of me felt like I was in a grotesque horror movie.

But then quietly, just above a whisper, my supervisor began talking about the woman's life. She told me where she was from, what she did, where her family lived, and how she died. As I stood there holding her hand, a transformation happened. The dead woman became a person to me. She was not just a dead body; she was the remains of a human being who had lived and loved and laughed and learned—a woman who had been loved by God and who would be missed by many. In that moment I began to feel as though I was holding something holy, as if this whole experience had just entered a sacred space. My heart opened to the presence of God in a way I seldom knew. God was undeniably present.

And in that sacred space, I sensed God speaking this into my spirit: "David, this is why I came. Everything you see here—this loss, this death, the physical end of this person—this is what I came to defeat through my Son, Jesus." Suddenly the resurrection became vitally important to me. The phrase *coming back to life* took on new meaning. I began to feel what I can only describe as a rage against the death that had claimed this woman, incensed that death had left her cold, lifeless, and empty. I was overwhelmed by the feeling that everything I was taking in, everything I was seeing and experiencing was *wrong*. This could not be how God intended it. This couldn't really be his plan, could it?

The answer, of course, is no. Death is and always will be a corruption of the perfect plan and will of God. God's original plan was a good plan for the fullness of life in the eternal abundance of relationship with him. Think back to Genesis 1:31. God has spoken creation into existence, and then in one breathtaking moment, he beholds what he has made and declares it *good*. That is the original plan, the plan before death and sin entered in, the plan as it was supposed to be. Fast-forward to Revelation 21. John sees "a new heaven and a new earth" (v. 1). He beholds the restoration of the original plan and declares, "He will wipe away every tear from their eyes. There will be no more death or mourning or crying or pain, for the old order of things has passed away" (v. 4).

Now there is death, but when the original plan is restored, there won't be any dying. And there won't be mourning or crying or pain. We are living in what will one day be the "old order." There will be a new order. Even so, we must live now in the consequences of what our rebellion from God ushered in. Therefore, every time we encounter moments like I had in that hospital room, we feel it and sense it deep in our souls. Our hearts cry out, *This can't be right. This cannot be what the living, loving God intended my life to be!*

Perhaps you remember the first time you came face-to-face with those feelings. I felt them so strongly as I walked around that hospital bed, and yet the woman in the bed was not even a relative or close friend. Still I felt that something was distinctly and eternally wrong. When death impacts us personally, when the person in the bed is our loved one or our friend, the feelings are multiplied many times over. We cry out to the Lord. It's as if we know that he alone can correct whatever it is that has gone horribly wrong.

I have heard too many parents say, "Mothers are not supposed to bury their children." I've heard too many spouses say, "I thought we would grow old together." I've heard too many close friends say, "How could such an accident happen?" Maybe you've felt that way too. They're actually saying,

God wanted me to raise my child.

God wanted me to live to old age with my wife.

God didn't want my friend to be hit by a drunk driver.

This wasn't supposed to be the plan!

Still, we have to fight those feelings of rage and anger. In times of grief or loss, anger is one of the most acute, raw human emotions we feel. There in those moments, we start looking for answers and ask the bigger, harder questions: Why did this have to happen? Why do I have to deal with this in the first place?

I know there are instances, especially in times of great pain or personal suffering, when death can be a relief; but most of the time, it's anything but. Most of the time, it just hurts. It's wrong. It's the reason we know, deep down, that death is our enemy. That is why we fear it. And yet if we are to conquer that fear and be encouraged by God's truth, we have to be willing to come near it. We have to walk around it, examine it, even touch it. We have to honestly encounter the reality of death and in so doing learn how to handle it so that our fears are tempered by the peace Christ and his resurrection promises.

The Beginning of Death

As we begin to draw close to something we regularly avoid, we need to grasp where death came from in order to understand how we move from it to life and hope.

While we may express it in different ways—often through pain or anger—we want to know *why* we have to endure death. From the time we're very young, we learn to come to terms with the fact that life ends. A young boy who loses his dog turns to his mother in tears and asks, "Why did Winnie have to die?" Eventually, we all ask the *why* questions: If God is good and he loves us, why can't life just go on as it is? Why do we have to lose those we love?

One of my colleagues, Donna McClellan, went through a tremendously difficult time as she cared for her dying mother. The ordeal began with several trips from Orlando to the Seattle area where her mother lived. Donna helped to arrange nursing and then hospice care, but when her mother reached a critical stage, she decided to stay to be at her mother's bedside. Given the progression of her mother's illness, Donna thought it would only be a matter of days, but it took weeks. Her mother was in great discomfort. She hardly ate. It was agonizing for Donna to watch. It seemed to go on and on. At one point, totally exhausted, Donna called me, and in a moment of pure honesty she said, "Why does this have to be so hard?" In essence, she was saying, "This is just wrong. Why does it have to be this way?"

Without a Christian worldview, it is hopeless to try to answer that question. It has no answers. But when we understand the question through the truth of God's Word, we can at least reach a place of understanding—and hope. The answer lies in the nature of our sinful, fallen world. Paul mentions it in 1 Corinthians 15:21–22. As he tries to explain the wonder of our immortality through Christ, he considers first the origins of death. The bad news comes before the good news. Paul writes, "Since death came through a man, the resurrection of the dead comes also through a man. For as in Adam all die, so in Christ all will be made alive." Paul is explaining to the Corinthian Christians how death came about in the beginning. Death, he says, came through a man. It is primarily an allusion to Adam, but all humankind is included.

Looking back at Genesis 1–3, we read that God is the Creator of the universe. Those chapters provide a brief but exhilarating description of the life-giving, creative power of God. He speaks and worlds are formed. Water and sky, sea and air, sun, moon, and stars—God creates, effortlessly, eternally. And his crowning achievement is humanity. Genesis 2:7 says, "The LORD God formed a man from the dust of the ground and breathed into his nostrils the breath of life, and the man became a living being." No other creature God made is described in that way. Human beings alone are *living beings*. He breathed his *life* into us in a way that corresponds to his nature, and in so doing, he gave us a quality of life unique from everything else. It's what makes us capable of being in relationship with God.

Once God created Adam, he was also quite clear about the parameters of his life, saying in Genesis 2:16–17, "You are free to eat from any tree in the garden; but you must not eat from the tree of the knowledge of good and evil, for when you eat from it you will certainly die." This passage thoroughly contradicts the notion that God ever intended us to *have it all*. Have you ever noticed that? Many of us have adopted the false notion that a good life is a life in which we deny ourselves nothing, a life in which we have everything we want. We sometimes mistakenly view God as the one who is supposed to give it to us.

Somehow, having it all becomes the goal. The reality is that no such thing was ever intended. God made it clear from the start that we could not have everything. We were not made to be our own gods, to have the knowledge of good and evil. Instead, we were created to be in relationship with God as his beloved sons and daughters. We are not capable of knowing what is truly good and what is truly evil. Who but God can honestly know the depths of these things? As finite human beings, such knowledge will destroy us.

Therefore, when we choose to deny that truth, death becomes a reality. Genesis 2:17 is the first mention of death. It's the consequence of our willful disobedience. You know the rest. Adam and Eve eat the fruit. They disobey God, and there are consequences to their disobedience. Their relationship with God fractures, and everything changes.

God created all things in a beautiful, holy way. Death had no part in it. But because man and woman chose to sin against a holy God, a price had to be paid. Part of God's holiness is justice. Disobedience has to be answered. God says,

> Because you listened to your wife and ate from the tree about which I commanded you, "You must not eat of it," cursed is the ground because of you. . . . By the sweat of your brow you will eat your food until you return to the ground, since from it you were taken; for dust you are and to dust you will return.
>
> Genesis 3:17, 19

God made the parameters painfully clear. We chose to go our own way, and we have been reaping the consequences of that choice ever since. The apostle Paul affirms this when he says, "For the wages of sin is death" (Rom. 6:23).

The consequence of our sin is that we forfeit the life God gave us. Period. It's cut and dried. There's no wiggle room. Apart from God, there is no life. We know instinctively that somewhere along the line something went horribly, irrevocably wrong. In his sermon "The Weight of Glory," C. S. Lewis describes it as "our inconsolable secret":

> We should hardly dare to ask that any notice be taken of ourselves. But we pine. The sense that in this universe we are treated as strangers, the longing to be acknowledged, to meet with some response, to bridge some chasm that yawns between us and reality, is part of our inconsolable secret. And surely, from this point of view, the promise of glory, in the sense described, becomes highly relevant to our deep desire. For glory meant good report with God, acceptance by God, response, acknowledgment, and welcome into the heart of things. The door on which we have been knocking all our lives will open at last.[1]

We have been knocking on the door all our life, trying to get in, trying to understand where this pain, death, and heartache came from. Our sin put us on the outside of that door. Our sin separated us from the life of the Father, and in the absence of the Father, there is no life. If God is the Author and Creator of life, then apart from him there is no life. God affirms that when he says through John that "in him [Jesus] was life, and that life was the light of all mankind" (John 1:4). If God is life and light, then when we choose to separate ourselves from God, the result is death and darkness. That is death's origin.

And yet in that same Genesis passage, something rather amazing happens. Yes, we see God's holiness, but we also see the depth of his tenderness and love—the first glimpse that although death has entered, ultimately it will not prevail. Genesis 3:21 says, "The LORD God made garments of skin for Adam and his wife and clothed them."

It is startling in its content. God declared death as the penalty for Adam and Eve's actions. After the chilling pronouncements of being buried in the earth and returning to dust, you expect that doom is certain. You expect God to come and blast them from the earth, but he doesn't. Instead, he gives us a picture of utter tenderness and love. This great God, this vast, limitless God who has just stretched out his hands to create the universe, now takes those same hands and makes clothes for Adam and Eve. The picture of the infinite God crafting two sets of tiny little garments is striking. It is an enormous symbol. Think about it. At that time, the only protection from the elements was what was on them—their clothing. Up until that point, until creation fell, protection wasn't needed. In essence, with this simple action God is saying, "I know you deserve death, but I am going to allow you to live—and I want to give you something that will protect you from the painful elements of this life." It is the first act of grace. They deserve death. Instead, God graciously gives them life.

Interestingly, it is also the first act of sacrifice. God had to take the life of a living animal, remove its skin, and craft it into something that could cover and protect his children. As his plan continued to unfold, animals were sacrificed and their blood became a *covering* for the sins of Israel. Think about the Passover and how the angel of death passed over any homes with door frames marked by blood. Ultimately, Jesus sacrificed his life, covering us with his blood and restoring us to right relationship with the Father. I find the unity of Scripture amazing, and here, in this one small sentence in Genesis, we see a foreshadowing of all the grace and sacrifice that is to come as God works out his plan for the world.

Christ came, he suffered real death, and yet he rose again. Thus, when we start to walk around the specter of death and face it in all its complexity, we must grasp its origins because they reveal the holiness of God's nature, the consequences of our sin, and yet God's ultimate plan to defeat it. From that truth, we find hope. In Christ, death never wins. Ever.

The Sting

Still, our hope in the resurrection of Jesus Christ does not take away death's hard reality. No matter how much we love the Lord or how deep our faith may be, death hurts. It stings. There is no getting around that. Yet somehow we've picked up this notion that if our faith is deep enough, death won't affect us in the same way. It won't wound as deeply or cut as sharply. Faith, we think, will immunize us against the poison of death's sting. We falsely believe that if we focus hard enough on the resurrection of our loved one through Christ, somehow we'll avoid the pain. No question, our reflection on the resurrection helps us. It encourages us, but it does not take away the fact that our loved one is gone. And that hurts.

In 1 Corinthians 15:55–56, Paul writes: "Where, O death, is your victory? Where, O death, is your sting? The sting of death is sin." Let's examine this passage. While Paul is declaring Christ's ultimate victory over death, his metaphorical use of the word *sting* draws on other scriptural references to the painful nature of death. The Greek word for *sting* is *kentron*, which is primarily used as a reference to the sting of insects and scorpions. Paul is clearly referencing that idea in these verses.[2] Understanding its full biblical meaning brings us closer to how deeply the sting of death can penetrate our life. Take note of how the *sting* is described in Revelation:

> And out of the smoke locusts came down on the earth and were given power like that of scorpions of the earth. They were told not to harm the grass of the earth or any plant or tree, but only those people who did not have the seal of God on their foreheads. They were not allowed to kill them but only to torture them for five months. And the agony they suffered was like that of the sting of a scorpion when it strikes. During those days people will seek death but will not find it; they will long to die, but death will elude them. . . . They [locusts] had tails with stingers like scorpions, and in their tails they had power to torment people.
>
> Revelation 9:3–6, 10

It's difficult to read—a gruesome word picture. And yet it's important that we appreciate the depth of its meaning. The *kentron*—the sting—was so painful that people sought death. That's the power of the word Paul uses in 1 Corinthians 15. The sting of death wounds us deeply. It can cause pain so vast that we no longer want to live. This is not the prick of an insect bite. This is a devastating, torturous wound. It is the *sting* of death.

Notice the intimate link between 1 Corinthians 15 and Revelation 9. Unlike the 1 Corinthians passage, Revelation 9 is not metaphorical. It's a description of actual pain and suffering, a future time when a painful reign of locusts and scorpions will come.[3] While I do not believe we are living in the time Revelation 9 describes, this passage is a sobering reminder that there are those living today who "seek death." Because of painful circumstances—medical issues, broken families, personal failures, crushing loneliness—people reach a point where they may actually *choose* death through suicide. Yet death is not to be sought, not because it won't provide some relief to the pain (indeed, it may very well do so), but because death has been conquered. We are immortal. Coping with the *sting* of death requires that we seek the balm Christ provides through his death and resurrection.

In all of Scripture, *kentron* is never used in a positive sense. It is always painful. To some degree, it always *tortures*. Death stings deeply and pervasively regardless of how it happens. My grandmother was a significant person to me who deeply impacted my childhood. During those formative years, she lived only four blocks away, allowing me almost unfettered access to this loving, giving person. She died two days after her ninetieth birthday when she went into her bathroom, picked up her toothbrush, and had a massive heart attack. The doctors told us she never knew what hit her. She was gone in an instant and felt no pain.

Compare that to my father-in-law, Dick Bywaters, who died at sixty-seven from a malignancy. My wife, Leigh, cared for him in his last week. It was slow and agonizing and painful and difficult. His death occurred in a completely different way than my grandmother's, but I can tell you that the sting was no different. Standing with my family at my grandmother's cemetery service, I'll never forget my mother's tear-streaked face as she said, "You are never ready to lose your mother." Though my grandmother's death was later in life, at what people consider a more *acceptable* age, and though she died quickly, that did not make her loss any less painful to me and my family than the sting of my father-in-law's death. It doesn't matter when or how it happens: death hurts. It's not helpful to suggest to someone that because his or her loved one died at an expected time or in an expected way that the sting is somehow dulled. It's not. That's not to say that losing a nine-year-old feels the same as losing someone who is ninety. The experience of grief is different, but both wound us nonetheless.

People need permission to acknowledge the sting of death and live into that pain. Here's where I think we miss it: sometimes faithful Christian men and women feel as though bearing faithful witness in grief means they must tell people, "I'm really doing fine. I know my loved one is in heaven, and it's really okay." It's as though we don't think it's okay to say, "This really hurts." The pressure to bear the appropriate witness makes us feel that if we cry, we will somehow disappoint God in how we handle our grief. No! Death hurts. It stings in a most torturous way. We need permission to say it and to feel it. When I walked around that woman's bed in the hospital that day, I needed my supervisor gently telling me, "It's okay to feel the feelings." Everything in me wanted to scream, "This is not right!" and I didn't even know the woman. Imagine how much more we want to scream in pain when we lose those we love.

We see this truth in the story of Lazarus in John 11. Mary and Martha send word to Jesus that their brother, Lazarus, is gravely ill. They ask him to come quickly. But by the time Jesus arrives, Lazarus is already dead. I love Mary's reaction to Jesus when he gets there. She responds in the same way many of us do when we pray over a loved one and that prayer goes unanswered. She says, "Lord, if you had been here, my brother would not have died" (John 11:32). It was a nice way of saying, "Where in the world were you? Why didn't you get here faster? Why didn't you do something? If you had just done what you're capable of doing, none of this would have happened."

John 11:33 continues the story: "When Jesus saw her weeping, and the Jews who had come along with her also weeping, he was deeply moved in spirit and troubled." And then in John 11:35, we find the tears of God: "Jesus wept." He was "deeply moved" (v. 33), which is another way of saying that Jesus felt the sting of

44

death as well. He looked at those he loved, Mary and Martha, and he saw how death had stung them too. The pain drew forth God's tears.

Here's what I find amazing: Jesus absolutely knew what he was about to do. He knew that in mere moments he would bring Lazarus back from death. He knew that, at least in that one moment, he was going to defeat death for that family, and yet he still felt the sting. He still knew death's pain. And so do we. We can know all about the promise of Easter. We can know every detail about the glory of heaven, but this side of that heaven, we still know death's sting. If Jesus knew it and he wept, then it's okay for us to know it too. We don't need to make a wooden affirmation that death does not wound us. You have God's permission to acknowledge the sting of death and the pain it creates in your life.

The Last Enemy

When I was in the seventh grade, I had the misfortune of getting on the wrong side of another boy in my class named Gordon. To be honest, I don't know the first thing about Gordon other than that he was in my class that year and he did not like me. I don't remember why he didn't like me, but for many weeks he waited for me after school and tried to beat me up. As much as I knew how to define it at the time, he was my enemy. Every day I had to create some strategy to deal with him because I knew he was going to be there. Barring some act of God, he was not going away.

Rest assured, I did all I could to avoid him. I cried to my parents. I tried to get them to let me stay home. I feigned being sick a few times. I wanted to run away from it, but deep down I knew that if I did that, I would actually be hurting myself. I was altering what I wanted to do—not taking part in the things that brought me joy—simply because an enemy lurked about. The only way I was ever going to get on with my life was to face my enemy. I had to acknowledge his presence. I had to accept the fact that he wanted to cause me pain in some way, and I had to deal with it.

I'm sure you're waiting for some great ending to this story. I wish I had one. I faced Gordon one day after school, and not only did he beat me up, but he also beat up one of my friends who came to defend me. In an odd sort of way, however, once we had faced him, he wasn't that scary anymore. I knew what he was. I felt his sting. Others became more aware of it and supported me in dealing with it. I learned a few things in the process. He was still my enemy, but I was better able to live my life without fear of his interference. Once he realized that he didn't scare me that much anymore, he started leaving me alone. He slowly faded because of one simple act: I faced him. I dealt with it.

Death is our enemy, and part of learning to live in this world where death still reigns and has the power to hurt us is to acknowledge that our enemy is real. We need not run from it. The only way we ever get back to the business of living is when we have honestly acknowledged and faced the enemy. When we do, the enemy does not seem so powerful anymore. The enemy is still there, but he fades somewhat in our consciousness. The enemy no longer dominates. Or perhaps we learn to live in its presence with more confidence. The quote from Henri Nouwen at the beginning of this chapter suggests that we can "befriend" death. I don't believe that Nouwen is suggesting friendship with death, as though we could somehow derive blessing from it. I think he means that in some small way, we can learn to face the enemy and make peace with his presence. It's not going away. Barring the return of Christ in our lifetime, we'll have to deal with it, so we lean into it. We face it.

Ever since my children were born, I have been writing them letters. I have a spiral notebook for each child, and every year on Christmas and their birthdays, I write them a letter. The plan is to give them their book of letters on their twenty-first birthday. I write to them about life, about things we have shared together in that particular time, about qualities or gifts that I observe in them, and about how I think God can use them. I write about the plan I see God unfolding for their lives, about funny moments we had together or vacations that were particularly special, about my own human frailties and the places where I have made mistakes. Mainly, though, it's my way of telling them over and over again that I love them, that I always have, and that I always will.

I will admit to you my great fear in writing those letters over the years. Every time I sit down with pen in hand, I think about the prospect that perhaps I will not get to finish the book. I fear that either they will not be here for their twenty-first birthday or I will not be here to place the book in their hands. Perhaps somewhere in the back of my mind, the letters are a hedge against my untimely death. Perhaps I started them because in the event of my sudden demise, they would still have something of me to remember, something of my words, counsel, and love. On several occasions while writing these letters, I have shed tears on the pages. Words fail me in describing the emotional nature of what those letters mean to me and what I hope they will mean to my children. But here's the thing: the thought that I may not be the one to give them the letters or that they may not ever receive them did not stop me from writing them. Yes, that last enemy is out there. I know where it comes from and why it exists. I know its sting. But through Christ, I choose to live. While I never know when or how I may be brought close to that enemy, I do not live in denial of its reality, nor do I allow its presence to overshadow the life I live.

On August 9, 2008, in the wake of several deaths she had experienced, Ellen Goodman wrote a column for the *Boston Globe* entitled "Nothing Is Forever." She describes the perilous nature of life and our attempts to hold on to it, like a vine that grows near her home:

> I wage war with bittersweet the way the old island farmers waged war with stones. When I temporarily beat back the enemy, I too declare victory—"There, done!"—then smile at my own arrogance. As if it were ever done. We create lives. Then nature, in its benign indifference, takes over, upending the illusion of power and permanence.[4]

Permanence is an illusion. We cannot keep back the tide. Goodman captures the reality we all must face, but that's not all there is. Death is real, but I live in the hope of Jesus Christ. I live in the hope of the empty tomb. I live in the security of a God who tenderly and graciously loves me, who empowers me to live between what is now and what is yet to come, and who has guaranteed my immortality with him in heaven. Like many things in life, there is tension between those realities. Death exists. It's not going away. That's real, and it's at the heart of the first part of our journey toward everlasting life, but I hold that in tension with the fact that Christ defeated death. Therefore, death will not ultimately defeat me. I am deeply and hopelessly darkened by sin, and there are consequences with that. Even so, I hold that in tension with the fact that I am more treasured and loved by God than I ever thought possible—a love demonstrated on the cross of Calvary. I'm not sure I can ever reach Nouwen's idea of "befriending death," but in Christ I have come to understand death in a new light. Death is a portal of sorts, that enemy I must encounter to move on to the glory that awaits me. If that is what is required, then I can make peace with that in the knowledge of Christ's resurrection, and in that truth, my perspective changes.

When we take the time to walk around death, we do not remove its existence, but we do gain an understanding that allows us to find the path of life. It allows us to keep living in the manner we have been called to live through Christ, not denying the pain of its sting, but resting in the arms of the one who eternally removed that sting and gave us victory.

2

How Do I Handle It?

Finding Assurance in Our Fears about Leaving This World

So we fix our eyes not on what is seen, but on what is unseen, since what is seen is temporary, but what is unseen is eternal.

2 Corinthians 4:18

I am not afraid of death. I just don't want to be there when it happens.

Woody Allen

Is there any meaning in my life that the inevitable death awaiting me does not destroy?

Leo Tolstoy, *A Confession*

I'll admit it. It really *did* scare me. I think anyone reading the form I had just been handed would have been at least a *little* scared.

Reading that form only added to the bizarre series of events that had unfolded over the previous few days.

It all started when I went out for a run, something I had done four or five days a week for fifteen years. I was in the third mile of a five-mile run when I suddenly felt a sharp pain in the right side of my chest, almost like being stabbed with a knife. Like any male, I rationalized that it was a stitch in my side—something that can happen to runners from time to time. I assumed it would pass, so I kept going. Well, it didn't. The longer I ran, the worse it got. I pushed through another mile, but when I started wheezing, I knew it was time to shut it down. I stopped running and started walking, still about a mile from my house.

As soon as I did that, the pain started to subside. *Ah*, I thought, *It's going away. I'm fine.* By the time I got home, there was no pain at all, but I could not shake the wheezing. It was hard to take a deep breath. I finally mentioned something to my wife, who encouraged me to call a doctor, which I did. The doctor heard my symptoms, asked a few more questions, and then told me to meet him at the ER. "Don't you think that's a little over the top, doctor?" I asked. He assured me it was not.

Several hours and a CT scan later, I was diagnosed with a partially collapsed right lung, which brought with it the added bonus of a large chest tube planted in the center of my right side. It was miserable. Doctors assured me the lung would repair itself over the course of a few days, but unfortunately, that did not happen. Twice they successfully reinflated my lung, but it didn't last. Within hours, the lung collapsed again. After three exasperating days, I was told I needed surgery to fix it.

Enter the form. I had been moved from my hospital room to the pre-op area where nurses get you ready for whatever procedure you're about to have. (I loved it when one nurse put a big purple X on my right side, ensuring that my doctor would operate on the correct lung. X marked the spot.) As I lay there admiring my new hospital gown, a different nurse came in asking me to sign some release forms. Since I had never been in that situation, I asked her, "What is this that I'm signing?" "Oh, it's standard stuff," she said.

Even so, I paused to read it before signing. Here's what jumped out at me:

> I understand the risks involved to my surgery include, but may not necessarily be limited to: bleeding, infection, death, stroke, renal failure, intestinal ischemia, extremity ischemia which may require amputation, heart attack, blood clot, persistent pain, pulmonary embolus, prolonged intubation, and other neurological damage.

Looking back on it, I think it's kind of funny how they sneak *death* in there at number three, as though that's somehow the third worst thing that can happen to you. "Bleeding, infection, death." On further review, they may want to move death up there to number one. There I sat, awaiting my surgery, and someone hands me a form that says, essentially, "You may die if you do this."

Maybe it was the vulnerability I was already feeling from the entire situation, but a wave of fear washed over me. I tried all the basic rationalizations to get rid of it. *The odds of that happening, David, are very small. These people do these operations every day. You'll be fine.* I even spiritualized it, thinking, *God will not let that happen to you, David. You're in his hands. He loves you.* But I could not get over the fear. I had been in too many hospitals and seen too many random surgical tragedies. Such outcomes were real possibilities. As I put my signature on that form, I felt I was entrusting my life to a group of people I barely knew. Needless to say, that was not a pleasant feeling.

You always wonder how you'll react in those sorts of situations. You can talk about death and your faith all you want, but you never really know how you'll react until you're in the moment where circumstances bring it especially near. To be clear, I know that in the back of my mind, I did not actually think I was going to die, but the prospect certainly came near. Staring at that form, I mentally entered into that space where death was a possibility. I lay there quietly, fear in my gut, thinking about things like what my wife and children would do without me, what it would feel like when I died, what or who I would see when I passed into the next life, if what I had done on earth mattered. I confess that I felt doubt. What if all that I had professed was not actually true? What if there's nothing?

I felt a crushing sadness that I would not be able to tell my parents or my sisters good-bye, talk to my close friends ever again, or walk my daughter down the aisle at her wedding. Tears welled up as I thought about never seeing my grandchildren or never growing old with my wife. And I thought about the prospect of seeing God. What if I die and in the next few hours I am standing before almighty God? What if this is really it?

Maybe some people in the world are so faithful and so attuned to God that when they come to those moments—even more realistic than mine—they are not afraid. Maybe they're so filled by the Spirit that those moments are bathed in total peace. Perhaps, but I think that is far more the exception than the rule. I think that as finite, flawed human beings, it is quite normal and natural to fear our demise. If it did not bother us in some way, I'm not sure we valued life to begin with.

Of course there are circumstances in which death is a welcome relief from pain and suffering. I have seen people in those situations who embrace the possibility and actually long for it. I am not denying those realities but simply acknowledging that for most of us, fear is a normal reaction to the prospect of death. And if it is, then the challenge is to examine those fears and not deny them.

If we superspiritualize our self-talk and externally exude the Christian bravado we think must accompany the life and manner of a *good Christian*, we only do ourselves and others a disservice. We prevent ourselves from looking honestly at why we fear death, never allowing the transparency needed to grow spiritually. We never allow the hope of God's answers to take root in us and grow. And if we don't grow, we have nothing to offer others around us who fear the same things and who may look to us for the hope they lack. Denying our fears only forces them deeper into an ever-widening pool of angst and anxiety. Facing the fears and considering God's Word in response to them brings the peace we so long for. And by examining those fears now, we make ourselves all the more ready for the inevitable moment that is to come.

Check Your Vision

Through the years of my ministry, I have spoken with many people who were either nearing death or at death's door, and in those moments I always inquire something like, "Tell me how you're feeling," or "Tell me about your faith right now—how is it?" What I have found is the amazing power of focus. If the person is focused on what is *down* and not on what is *up*, there is great fear and anxiety. When they focus on the reverse, peace ensues. When people focus on just the physical, their mind and attention are so riveted on it that they cannot grasp the spiritual. Essentially, they are not allowing what is spiritually and eternally true to impact how they view their current physical reality. Psalm 121:1–2 reminds us: "I lift up my eyes to the mountains—where does my help come from? My help comes from the LORD, the Maker of heaven and earth."

Too often we cast our gaze on the physical and not up to the place where we find our help. Paul speaks to this in 2 Corinthians 4:16–18:

> Therefore we do not lose heart. Though outwardly we are wasting away, yet inwardly we are being renewed day by day. For our light and momentary troubles are achieving for us an eternal glory that far outweighs them all. So we fix our eyes not on what is seen, but on what is unseen, since what is seen is temporary, but what is unseen is eternal.

He tells us not to lose heart, because there is a reality other than the one we see. The seen physical realm is only temporary. The unseen spiritual realm, governed by God, is actually the dominant, eternal one in which we will find a life so rich and full that all manner of suffering in this life will be forgotten. In facing our fears, we view them through a gaze lifted to the Father, lifted to the truth and the hope of his Word. We view our fears through the lens of God's answers.

As much as I believe this to be true, I also acknowledge the very real power of physical suffering. When you're experiencing great physical pain or discomfort, or battling just to take a breath, it is very difficult to focus on anything other than the physical. I'm not suggesting that by lifting our eyes to heaven we can magically whisk away the damnable consequences of cancerous tumors or neuromuscular diseases. God does not promise to remove us from our suffering, but he does promise us his presence in it. I believe that even in the physical suffering that may precede death, we can find the spiritual peace we long for—a peace that brings deep comfort even in the midst of physical strife.

One of my dear friends in the church was diagnosed with mesothelioma and died in just a few short weeks. It was agonizing and painful, but he taught me so much about spiritual peace even in the midst of suffering. Every day when I entered his hospital room, I found him immersed in reading Scripture and singing hymns. He was absolutely intentional about his spiritual focus, and the result was a spiritual joy I have rarely seen in people in his situation. Yes, he was suffering physically, but that did not preclude him from experiencing the peace and joy of God.

Thus, as I pray with and for others, no matter the suffering, I remind them to lift their gaze, to raise their heads so they can see beyond what is here and now and to remember the one who is sovereign over all things, the Redeemer and Ruler of the world.

Exploring Our Fears

While our fears about death are wide and varied, I have found that they can be grouped into a fairly tight series of questions that when answered can open our hearts to the deep truths of God that bring profound and lasting comfort. I do not pretend to think the list of questions I address in this chapter is by any means exhaustive, but I think they do help us get at the heart of some of our most basic fears.

Question 1: Will I Have Enough Faith?

None of us know exactly when death will come for us or for those we love, but just as I did in that operating room, we do *try it on* from time to time. I have not lost either of my parents, but my wife's father passed away several years ago. When she talks about missing her father or memories of her father, I often wonder, *What will that be like when it happens to me? How will I respond to it? Will I be able to speak at the service? Will I be able to compose myself enough to talk to their friends and mine?* Essentially, I'm wondering whether my faith will afford me the strength to face that loss and persevere through it. Will my faith be enough? We wonder about it in that context, and when considering our own death, we wonder about it even more.

When we receive a diagnosis that makes the reality of our death more likely, or when we *try it on* through watching a loved one get such a diagnosis, one of our deep fears is that somehow the faith we have professed all our lives will be found wanting. We fear that when we get the news, we will collapse into a weeping mass of anxiety, unable to face what is before us or to engage those whom we love in a way that truly reflects our faith in Christ. I have encountered many people who say to me with great disappointment, "I thought I would have been stronger." They feel a great sense of guilt that their faith was not the rock they thought it would be.

In those moments, I always go back to Thomas. In John 14, Jesus tenderly explains his pending departure and the glorious hope that there is a place prepared in heaven for those who are his disciples. Thomas, in a moment of fear, blurts out, "Lord, we don't know where you are going, so how can we know the way?" (v. 5). Showing him no condemnation, Jesus reassures Thomas of what he already knows, saying, "I am the way and the truth and the life" (v. 6). Fear can at times overwhelm what we already know. In those moments, we return to the gentle voice of our Savior, reminding us again and again of what we already know: Jesus is the Way, and in the end, he will be faithful to his promises.

Consider also the oft-forgotten truth that Thomas was among the disciples who, following the day of Pentecost, went out into the world, boldly proclaiming the truth of Jesus Christ. Because of Thomas's life, I never think it's all one thing or the other. When we wonder if our faith will be enough or if we will doubt, I think we realize that as human beings, it will most likely be both. Like Thomas, we will have moments of doubt and fear, but we will also have moments of great boldness and strength.

Further, we need never fear that we somehow lack the right *amount* of faith. Jesus said in Matthew 17:20, "If you have faith as small as a mustard seed, you can say to this mountain, 'Move from here to there,' and it will move. Nothing will be impossible for you." Paul writes in Romans 12:3, "Think of yourself with sober judgment, in accordance with the faith God has distributed to each of you." We must remember that faith is not something we generate ourselves. It is given to us by God. Therefore, wondering whether we *have enough* faith suggests that God will somehow shortchange us. To the contrary! God is the author and perfecter of our faith (Heb. 12:2), and as such, what he gives us will always be sufficient, even to the point of moving mountains if necessary.

When you face a crisis of faith or wonder whether you will have enough, remember you are human. Like Thomas, you will have some fearful moments, but as you focus on the object of your faith and allow God's Word to fill you, I believe you will become the Thomas of Acts: strong and standing firm, boldly living out the faith you profess even in life's most challenging circumstances.

Question 2: Will God Really Forgive Me?

In most of our day-to-day lives, we give little thought to the sheer majesty and glory of God. We don't linger much on the reality that he is far beyond anything our little brains can conceive, that his power is matchless; his holiness, complete; his purity, inapproachable. When we think about our death, however, those qualities quickly come into sharp focus. No matter how faithful we may have been in this life, no matter how many times we went to church or how kindly we may have tried to treat others, we wonder, *Will it be enough? Will God consider me worthy?* When honestly compared to God's nature, we fear the answer. Knowing what we know about how we have lived, we wonder, *How can God possibly forgive me? Will he?*

The flaw in this line of questioning is that we assume the answer lies with us. It doesn't. Whether God will forgive us has nothing to do with us and everything to do with Jesus. Paul reminds us in Ephesians 2:8–9, "For it is by grace you have been saved, through faith—and this is not from yourselves, it is the gift of God—not by works, so that no one can boast." Whether God will forgive us has nothing to do with what we did or didn't do, what we said or didn't say. It has everything to do with the central moment in Christianity, the fork in the road of human history: the cross of Jesus Christ.

Let me tell you about the unusual life of Lieutenant Hiroo Onada. As the Japanese army was evacuated from the Philippine islands on December 25, 1944, Onada's superiors left him behind, along with three other soldiers, to execute the following order: carry on the mission even if Japan surrenders.[1] One of those soldiers surrendered in 1950. Another died in a skirmish with local police in 1954. A third was found dead in 1972. Onada, however, continued to fight on, ignoring messages broadcast from loud speakers and leaflets dropped in the jungles, all assuring him that the war was over and he was free to come out. Living off the land and stealing food from the crops of local farmers, Onada finally surrendered on March 9, 1974. Even though the war was over, Onada still lived a life of great hardship and suffering. Because he did not grasp that the war had ended, Onada never allowed himself a moment of peace or rest.

What an apt description for how we live our lives at times. We simply cannot believe that Christ's work on the cross has completed the act of God's forgiveness—God's salvation—in our lives. As I said in the last chapter, the wages of sin are death, but God has accepted the death of Christ in place of our own. Through the righteousness imputed to us by the cleansing blood of Christ, we stand before God, the Father, as his redeemed. Christ has atoned, completely, for our sins. In John 19:30 Jesus said, "It is finished." It *is* finished. It is *finished*. That is the Good News of the gospel. Just like Lieutenant Onada, we desperately need someone to tell us when it's over, and that's what God in Christ has done. The work of your forgiveness has been completed. It's over. There's nothing else you need to do!

Looking at it a bit more closely, the Greek word for "finished" is *telestai*, derived from *telos*, which means "design or plan." The verb tense in John 19:30 is the perfect tense, meaning it is a perfect, completed action. Jesus is saying, "I've done it! The plan has been perfected! I've completed the plan!" His words don't refer to the end of his suffering; they are all about the work he has done for us. The perfect plan of God to forgive us and redeem us from our sins has been completed. Isaiah 53:5 proclaims, "The punishment that brought us peace was on him, and by his wounds we are healed." We have been spiritually and eternally healed by the wounds of Christ. We don't need to do anything else.

The problem with that, of course, is that we struggle to believe it. Something in our human nature says, "Surely there must be something I have to do to earn this." Grace runs so completely contrary to everything we experience in this life that it almost feels too good to be true. This is illustrated beautifully in 2 Kings 5 when Naaman, a great and mighty commander in the army of Aram, went to Elijah to be healed of his leprosy. Elijah instructed him to wash in the Jordan River seven times and he would be healed. But Naaman "went away angry" (v. 11). He was a great and mighty warrior, ready to do some great thing to win his healing; he could not grasp how simple it actually was. In the same way, we exclaim with Naaman, "It can't be that easy! Surely there must be more! If I don't do something meritorious, how can God forgive me?" Answer: You didn't do the meritorious work. Christ did. So go and be forgiven.

In the end, this is the beauty of Christian faith. Every other religious tradition in the world suggests that something must be done to merit God's favor. We have to dress or pray in a certain way or reach a certain level of consciousness or appease a series of gods. We have to make ourselves worthy enough to merit God's attention. It is *our* work. As Buddha said, "Strive without ceasing."[2] Jesus Christ comes and essentially says, "Stop it. Stop striving. I've done it. It's over."

When we come near to seeing God and we fear that somehow he won't forgive us, we need only remember a hill called Golgotha and a cross. We need only remember the sound of whips cracking and nails being hammered. We need only remember that Christ did for us what we could never do for ourselves. He became the propitiation (to appease or turn away wrath) for our sins. When I remind people of this, they often say, "But David, you don't know what I did. You don't know about this moment or that moment." To make such a comment is to say that the cross of Christ is not enough or that somehow Christ did not hang long enough or bleed enough for you. No! Paul declares in Romans 5:20, "Where sin abounded, grace abounded much more" (NKJV). Your sin can never exceed God's grace!

Therefore we know we can approach God's throne of grace with confidence. In this life or the next, we can come before God in the certain hope of our forgiveness. Hebrews 10:19, 21–22 declares, "Therefore, brothers and sisters, since we have confidence to enter the Most Holy Place by the blood of Jesus, . . . let us draw near to God with a sincere heart and with the full assurance that faith brings, having our hearts sprinkled to cleanse us from a guilty conscience." It is Christ's blood that sprinkles us and cleanses us. It is Christ's blood that assures our forgiveness. Therefore we approach the throne of God with *confidence, not fear.*

Still, somewhere in the back of our minds is this doubt that while God may love us, he does not really like us very much. When it comes down to it, he may yet reject us. In those moments of doubt, I always recall Zephaniah 3:17: "The LORD your God is with you, the Mighty Warrior who saves. He will take great delight in you; in his love he will no longer rebuke you, but will rejoice over you with singing." By God's grace, poured out on us in Jesus, God delights in us.

God is not waiting in heaven to smash you to pieces; he waits to usher you to that place he has prepared for you from the foundations of the world. Even now, the living God takes such joy in your life that he sings over you. He *sings* over you. So when you draw near to death, whenever that may be, you don't need to fear that you have not done enough. You only need to hear the gentle melody of the Savior's voice as he proclaims, "It is finished, my child. It is finished!"

Question 3: Is It Okay to Die?

I never cease to be amazed by the will of the human spirit to live. I have seen people who appear unable to draw one more breath fight on for days until a particular loved one arrives. I have seen people determined to spend one more Christmas with their family, and in spite of overwhelming physical odds, they live until that day. The human instinct to live—to survive—is beyond measure, a force that defies explanation.

That same instinct to live, however, can create a conundrum in our spirit. Because we have such an innate instinct to live, we can falsely believe that it is somehow morally wrong, or against God's will, to die. Thus, we fear letting go. We fear giving ourselves permission to stop fighting and trust our life into the hands of God.

Several months ago I visited an elderly woman in our congregation who had terminal lung cancer. She was one of those people whom pastors love—always present, always positive, always ready with an encouraging word. When I got to her house, I found her family somewhat shaken because she was experiencing significant pain. She seemed unable to rest and anxious in her spirit. While words were few and communication was difficult, I could see a look of fear on her face.

When I began to speak to her, I used words from Scripture filled with promises of peace and love. As those words washed over her, she began to calm somewhat, and she also seemed more able to listen. I told her what a faithful life she had led. I told her that God was pleased with her, that he took great delight in her as his daughter, and that he was ready to receive her into his kingdom. I said, "You have finished your race. It's okay. You can go home now." We prayed together for a while, and then I left. The next day, her family called to say that she had died. Though they grieved for her, they were grateful she had finally found a place of rest in her struggle.

Experiences like that happen over and over again. People fight and fight until someone gives them permission to let go. My dear friend Tom Devor fought a courageous battle with AIDS. At the end he weighed less than one hundred pounds, he was barely recognizable, and he was unconscious and unable to communicate; but somehow, he fought on. As he wheezed and gasped for air, I'll never forget bending down and whispering in his ear, "Tom, God loves you. It's okay now. You can go. I'm here with your mother. She's going to be fine. We'll see you later." He had been fighting like that for days, yet when he heard those words, within moments he was gone.

As we face our own fears of dying, and as we care for others who face that prospect, we all need to be reminded of God's plan. There is a time when our physical life ends. We aren't doing anything wrong in God's eyes by accepting it. God's Word declares in Ecclesiastes 3:1–2, "There is a time for everything, and a season for every activity under the heavens: a time to be born and a time to die." We don't necessarily embrace or desire the time to die, but there is one, and when it comes, we need not deny it or feel guilty it has arrived.

Matthew 16 gives us another important passage when Jesus bluntly tells his disciples about his pending death. Peter responds by saying, "Never, Lord! . . . This shall never happen to you!" Jesus answers, "Get behind me, Satan! You are a stumbling block to me" (vv. 22–23). Jesus had an appointed time to physically die, as we all do. When Peter tried to deny that truth, Jesus rebuked him. When our appointed time comes, we need not try to deny it. By doing so, we can actually become a stumbling block to the unfolding plan of God in our life or the life of another. Because our instinct to fight is so strong, we often need to remind ourselves and others of this truth.

To be clear, I am not suggesting that we give up or not fight for life. Far from it. Life is a gift we have received from God, and as long as we draw breath, God has a purpose and a plan for our existence. Woven into that same plan, however, is the time for dying; and when it comes, we can be freed from the notion that resting in the arms of God is wrong. When it is our time, it's our time, and we trust in God's faithfulness to receive us into heaven.

Question 4: What about Those I Leave Behind?

From a purely human perspective, this may be the most prevalent fear of all. I find many people are relatively content with the prospect of their own death. What they cannot let go of is the fear of what will become of their loved ones in their absence. Life insurance agents love this fear. It's more than deep sadness over missing milestone events or experiences. It's a genuine fear that somehow the lives of their loved ones will be compromised.

I remember a day during my ministry in Chattanooga when I went alone to pray in the chapel of our church. We had three children who were three or younger, so things were a little nuts in our house. I was a young father, thirty-one years old, and to be honest, the prospect of raising three children and providing for all their needs was overwhelming. As I sat in the chapel praying, I began feeling a deep dread about what could happen to my wife and children if I died. I implored the Lord, "Please, please, whatever you do, let me see my children grow up. Let them have a father into their adulthood."

A few more days passed, but I still could not shake it. Back in that same chapel, now crying, I continued to plead with God, "Lord, I fear that I am going to die too young. My children need me. Please, God, don't let that happen." I know the fear was irrational. There was nothing in my life or personal health to suggest I would die any sooner than anyone else, but seeing the vulnerability of my young family kept those fears churning. Finally, sitting in that same chapel a few days later, I came to Psalms 22 and 25. Frankly, the Lord hit me over the head with them.

David declares in Psalm 22:30–31, "Future generations will be told about the Lord. They will proclaim his righteousness, declaring to a people yet unborn." I was struck by the reality that God has a multigenerational plan and was reminded that God was already planning for what will happen in my family generations after me.

I cannot tell you how significant that was to me. God was already planning for members of my family whom I will never even know! As I felt that reassurance, peace started to grow in me.

Then I came to Psalm 25:1–2: "To you, O LORD, I lift up my soul. O my God, in you I trust" (ESV). There I was, worried sick about my young family and what could happen to them if I died, and God presented me with a basic question: *Do you trust me?* I began praying, "Yes, Lord, I trust you. To you, I lift up my soul." A few verses later God really got me. The psalmist writes, "Who, then, are those who fear the LORD? He will instruct them in the ways they should choose. They will spend their days in prosperity, and their descendants will inherit the land" (Ps. 25:12–13).

To fully appreciate the magnitude of that passage, you have to understand the significance of "the land" in the Old Testament. When God made his covenant with Israel, it was based on the land he promised to give them. The land was the sign of God's covenant. Thus, when David says that "their descendants will inherit the land," it is more than just property. It is God's way of saying that the children of those who are faithful to the Lord will inherit the covenant of God—his promise. God will be faithful.

In that moment, I felt a wave of relief wash over me as I considered the folly of my own arrogance. I had been acting as though my life was indispensable to the plan of God in the lives of my children. How arrogant of me to assume that I was necessary to God accomplishing his will and plan for their lives! The sovereign plan of God for my life does not exclude the lives of my wife or my children. If in the sovereignty of his will it is my time to die, then included in that is his plan for the lives of my children, a plan that included my death.

Put in its simplest form, if God is the supreme and holy Creator of all people, and he lovingly cares for us each day, then how can I possibly assume he will be unable to care for my children and my wife in my absence? I can't. God will care for those I love. Thus, I go back to Psalm 25:1–2: I lift up my soul, and I trust in God. I remind myself of the magnitude and power of his nature, and I rest in the knowledge that he will enact his plan for my loved ones and graciously care for them, whether I am present in their lives or not.

Question 5: Did My Life Make a Difference?

Deep in every human heart is the question of significance. We want our life to matter, to count for something more in the grand scheme of things than just the fact that we used up some oxygen over seventy-five years. Especially in cases where illness leads someone gradually toward death, that person has ample moments to consider the merits of his or her life, and any regrets as well. Many will do an evaluation, and depending on the circumstances, they may fear their life made no difference, that somehow they did it wrong. They fear they were given one shot at life and they failed. Left unchecked, those fears can be crushing.

Again, this is where God's answers found in Scripture are so critical. Psalm 33:11 declares, "The plans of the LORD stand firm forever, the purposes of his heart through all generations." When we fear that our life did not matter or that we did not have the impact we hoped, it's helpful to be reminded that God's plan and purpose for us is never thwarted. The plan of God will always prevail, and while the events or circumstances may not have gone according to our plan, God's purpose for our life is not thwarted. God made us with a purpose and a plan, and according to his sovereign will, that plan will be fulfilled. Death cannot destroy that purpose. God's purposes stand firm forever.

We also are not really in the position to know our life's impact. Paul writes in 1 Corinthians 13:12, "For now we see in a mirror dimly, but then face to face. Now I know in part; then I shall know fully" (ESV). This side of heaven, we can scarcely imagine the way in which God uses our life to enact his good and perfect will. It's like looking in a foggy mirror. We can only see blurred images. But when we enter into God's heavenly kingdom, then we will know. God will show us all the ways he took our life and our actions, even our sinful choices and mistakes, and wove them together according to his purpose so that he was glorified. We don't need to know whether our life mattered. It is simply not something the human heart can quantify. All we need to know is Christ, and Christ crucified. What God does with our life is in his hands, so we trust him with the measure of its outcome.

I think that is the appropriate theme on which to end this chapter: *trust*. The antidote to fear is often trust, born out of the truth of God's Word, confirmed in us by his Holy Spirit. In our fears, we look not to what is physical but to what is beyond the physical. We look up to our loving, redeeming God. When C. S. Lewis came to the end of his epic Chronicles of Narnia series, he wrote one of the most comforting lines about this life and the next I have ever found, one that soothes my fears even now. In the last few lines of *The Last Battle*, he writes:

> And for us, this is the end of all the stories, and we can most truly say that they all lived happily ever after. But for them it was only the beginning of the real story. All their life in this world and all their adventures in Narnia had only been the cover and the title page: now, at last, they were beginning Chapter One of the Great Story, which no one on earth has read: which goes on forever: in which every chapter is better than the one before.[3]

All that consumes us in this life, the many things that we think matter so very much, are but the cover and the title page. The journey of our life in God has barely even begun here. We can appease our fears when we trust in God's Great Story, the one he is writing even now for our life, the one in which every chapter gets better than the one before as we eternally reside in his kingdom in the joy of our everlasting life. How I long for that next chapter to unfold.

3

What Do I Say? What Do I Do?

Ministry to Others through Death, Grief, and Loss

Carry each other's burdens, and in this way you will
fulfill the law of Christ.

Galatians 6:2

We still love life, but I do not think that death can take
us by surprise now.

Dietrich Bonhoeffer

I don't know what most people say at these occasions
because in all honesty, I've tried to avoid them.

Edward Cole, *The Bucket List*

Sometimes, there just aren't words.

I don't remember much about the day other than it was early.
I had dropped my kids off at school and headed to the office as

I always did. I was about halfway through my first cup of coffee when I got a frantic call about a terrible car accident east of the city. Sarah (not her real name), a young mother, had been on the way to drop off her daughter at school when another vehicle crashed into the passenger side of her car—the side where her daughter was sitting. In spite of her seat belt, the force of the crash ejected the five-year-old girl from the car. She was pronounced dead at the scene. Sarah, severely injured, was rushed to the local level-one trauma hospital.

I arrived shortly thereafter to find friends and family members enveloped by the shock of such tragedy. Many of the other mothers were crying. Some were on their cell phones. Low murmurs of conversation could be heard throughout the waiting area. It was chaotic, but in a quiet, almost dignified manner. I did not know Sarah or the father well, but they had been to my church a time or two, and I was the de facto pastor in their lives at that moment. I made my way to the desk, inquired about her condition, and asked if I could go see her. I was escorted back to a large trauma room with more machines and monitors than I had ever seen. Sarah was in the bed, her face so badly bruised and swollen that she was almost unrecognizable. Her husband sat quietly beside her, holding her hand, head down. Her mother and sister were alternately sitting and then pacing, overwhelmed by the magnitude of all that had happened.

It was not the first trauma room I had ever entered, but it ranked right up there as one of the most tragic. The question loomed in my mind: *What can I possibly say that would make any difference right now?* Words felt ridiculously inadequate, so I offered only a few. Instead, I moved from person to person, hugging each one, occasionally squeezing a hand, until I finally reached the bedside. Sarah had suffered serious physical injuries, including broken ribs and a shattered shoulder. Significantly medicated but still conscious, she stared blankly at the ceiling. I leaned down and whispered, "I am so very sorry about Ally" (not her real name). I gently squeezed her hand as I said it, and then I watched the tears begin to leak from both eyes, trickling down to the pillow beneath, her head never moving, her gaze never leaving the ceiling above.

Even with the acutely painful nature of the physical injuries she had sustained, I knew her physical pain paled in comparison to the emotional agony of losing her daughter. Every ounce of life seemed to have run out of her.

In the following days, Sarah gradually improved, at least to the point of going home. Because of her injuries, we delayed her daughter's funeral for almost a week, but even then, she could only manage it by staying in a wheelchair, almost motionless. I did my best to speak words of hope and comfort at the service, and then we moved to the cemetery for the burial. In spite of the distance there, many still came. We huddled around the plot as I shared Scripture and prayed.

What made the next few minutes a bit unusual was the fact that almost no one had seen Sarah since the accident. She had been in no condition to receive visitors, so people at the burial were anxious to speak to her. A line quickly formed at her wheelchair, and because she was in such a weakened state, I tried to stay close to her, knowing what could be coming. And sure enough, it did.

I know people mean well, but sometimes in their desire to say something comforting, they don't realize their words are anything but. The first person who reached Sarah said, "Well, God reached down and picked a rose for his garden, sweet lady." Sarah nodded, but the look on her face was that of one who had just been stabbed. A few more passed, and then I heard someone say, "I know how hard this is—my aunt passed last year." Then there was the ever popular "Ally is a little angel now" comment. On and on it went until Sarah could not take it any longer. It was just too much, so we moved her out of the line and into a waiting car.

Weeks later Sarah and I spoke about the things people had said. When grief is fresh and raw, as it was for her that day, reactions are stronger and more emotional. In time Sarah was able to reconcile in her mind the true intentions of those who came to see her. She knew they meant no harm, but the words were still piercing all the same. To suggest God *picked* her daughter for a garden implies that God ruthlessly and coldly took her without any care or consideration of Sarah's feelings. Our God, who is self-existent, has no need of anyone or anything. To suggest that God needed a child for his garden violates what we know to be true of his nature. Hearing such a comment only stirs anger at God or the speaker for asserting something so heartless.

Trying to assure someone that you "understand" how they feel is of little, if any, comfort. One person's experience with grief is never the same as anyone else's. Telling someone that you "know how it feels" only creates an internal response: *You could not possibly know how I feel! Losing your aunt is* not *the same thing as losing my daughter!*

And the "angel" comment, while popular, is not biblically or theologically correct. Angels are created in an entirely different manner than human beings, and human beings do not *graduate* to become angels. The danger in angel comparisons is that grieving people can begin to feel that their deceased loved one is somehow *watching over them* when that is not true. The person who watches over them is Christ, and any attachment to a lost loved one as guardian angel only impedes recovery.

From this one example, I hope you can see how important it is for us to think through how we care for others as they approach death or when they experience the loss of a loved one. As I said, I do not believe people intentionally say or do the wrong thing. I think things are said and done simply out of ignorance, and if we take the time to prepare, we can correct those errors and be much more effective at caring for those in need.

The Beauty of the Church

As a pastor, I am sure that the body of Christ, his church, is never more fully on display than when a person approaches death or when a person has just lost a loved one. I am always encouraged when I enter the hospital room of a terminally ill patient and find elders, deacons, or church members already gathered with that person in prayer, already supporting the rest of the family, already praying and communicating God's love. I am always encouraged when I go to the home of a family who has endured tragic loss and find that it is full of church members (most of whom lovingly brought casseroles—another church tradition!). I often say that the church is at her best in times of grief.

There is a reason for that. It is the same way that God expresses his relationship with us, and it is the way he calls us to love and care for others. The very name of Jesus, Emmanuel, means "God with us." In the pain and sin of our life, God comes to us in relationship. He comes to love and care and to help us bear the burden of this life. He comes to ultimately give us victory over those very things by his cross. This is the same way he calls the body to function.

First Corinthians 12:27 reminds us that whenever we come to faith in Christ, we become part of a body. Paul doesn't suggest that we take time to think about it or pray about whether we want to be part of the body. He simply says, "Each one of you is a part of it." When you come to faith in Christ, you're in, period. As members of the body, then, we also have responsibility for each other. We are called into a community to live not for our own ends but for the greater good of the kingdom of God.

Part of that is taking care of each other. Paul articulates this in Galatians 6:2 as he describes the ethical responsibilities inherent to being a member of the body of Christ. He writes, "Carry each other's burdens, and in this way you will fulfill the law of Christ." What is the law of Christ? Jesus sums it up in Matthew 22:37, saying essentially, "Love God and love others." In John 15:12, he says, "My command is this: Love each other as I have loved you." How has Jesus loved us? Christ helps us bear the burden of sin and death. Part of how we love others is helping them bear those same burdens.

You don't want to confuse this, though, with the old manner of keeping God's law, referred to in Matthew 18:21. Peter asks Jesus, "How many times shall I forgive my brother or sister who sins against me? Up to seven times?" That's a legalistic, rule-following question. We can't ask, "How many times must I care for someone who is grieving until I fulfill my obligation?" It's not a question of the law; it's a question of the heart. Jesus ushered in something totally different regarding life in the body of Christ. It's not about keeping the law to appease God. It's about love. It's about loving others as we have been loved. Therefore, when we go to the beds of the dying or the homes of the grieving, we do so not out of duty or moral obligation but because we know deep down that God has lovingly borne our burdens first. We go with his love poured into us by his Holy Spirit.

Understanding Grief

With that compelling call of the Lord within us, it is still important that we recognize the context of such ministry. When we go to comfort those who are grieving or to be with someone who is approaching death's door, we have to remember that they are dealing with very distinct issues and feelings. Each context we enter will be different. Part of having an impact as we serve is being prepared for *how* we serve.

While grief happens differently for each person, it is helpful to know at least some of the elements. In her well-known book, *On Death and Dying*, Elisabeth Kübler-Ross summarizes the various stages of grief:

denial and isolation

anger

bargaining

depression

acceptance[1]

Remember that not all people go through these stages sequentially, but they may move between them over time. I'm not necessarily trying to explain each stage or to make you an expert on the stages of grief. You don't need to be a grief recovery expert to extend the ministry of Christ. For those we encounter who may be in need of more assistance, we can refer them to mental health professionals who are more than equipped to provide helpful, expert care. We don't need to think of ourselves as amateur psychologists when we enter the room. In fact, that can be detrimental. Our task is to carry the hope and comfort of Christ, to listen, and to allow some of their burden to be cast on us through Christ.

That said, having an awareness of what the stages are and where a person may be at any given time can be helpful. Talking to someone only moments after a terminal diagnosis or hours after their loved one has died will be completely different from talking to them months after their diagnosis or loss. Their process will have brought them down a path of grief, and we need to be sensitive to those dynamics. For example, if a person is mad about their illness, then you need to listen to those feelings of anger and validate them. If a person is trying to bargain with God for more time, it's not helpful to say, "Oh, you're in the bargaining phase." It *is* helpful for you to know the stage exists and then to care for the person appropriately. Don't try to talk people out of where they are. It's not helpful to say, "I think you are denying the reality of your husband's death," but rather, "I can't believe that John is actually gone. I'm sure you feel like he's going to come walking in that door at any moment. It's hard to get used to, isn't it?" Again, our task is to help bear the burden and offer the hope and peace of Jesus.

In light of these tasks, it's important to recognize the central tools we have as we serve: prayer and Scripture. People get themselves in trouble and say the wrong thing because their mind goes blank in the moment. Fearing the silence, they blurt out something, usually something that makes no sense or wounds unintentionally. One of the most important things you can do is prepare yourself with Scripture. You don't have to memorize it or act like a Bible scholar. Just have something picked out and marked in your Bible. When you reach a place of silence or when you have moved through appropriate small talk, you can offer, "Joan, I was thinking about you today and I thought of this Scripture. May I read it to you?" God's Word is always appropriate in filling a void and in providing comfort. Consider these verses I've used in my ministry:

Psalm 23

Psalm 121

Psalm 139

Isaiah 40:29–31

Isaiah 43:1–4

Jeremiah 29:11

Zephaniah 3:17

John 14:1–6

John 14:27

Philippians 4:4–7

The ministry of prayer is also important. As you listen to someone share, make mental notes of what you will pray about later. If you have time to read Scripture, or even without it, earnestly ask, "Bill, may I pray for you?" Prayer is always a welcome ministry that gives strength in weakness. If you do not feel comfortable praying out loud, then you may want to use the Lord's Prayer, or you may want to pray through one of the Psalms. Scripture prayers can often provide a guide that gives us more security and confidence as we pray.

I want to bring one more very important point to your attention. When you're visiting people who are dying, they may move in and out of consciousness. At times they will be lucid; at other times it will appear as though they are not. In spite of that, never *talk over* unconscious people as if they are not there. Even if it appears they cannot hear you, speak to them. Tell them you are there. Whisper in their ear. Tell them you love them. Speak God's presence. Psalm 42:7 reminds us, "Deep calls to deep at the roar of your waterfalls." Paul affirms, "The Spirit himself intercedes for us with groanings too deep for words" (Rom. 8:26 ESV).

We must always remember that there is a spiritual world operating around us that we cannot see or fully understand, but one that is enormously powerful in moments of grief and death. Simply because we think a person cannot physically hear us does not mean that the Holy Spirit cannot minister to him or her from deep to deep (Ps. 42:7), interceding in ways that words cannot express. I have had far too many moments when supposedly unconscious people have suddenly looked me in the eye and spoken to ever doubt what may be happening in their heart or just below the level of human consciousness. Do not underestimate the ministry of the Holy Spirit through you.

The Ministry of Presence

As you can tell by now, one of the most powerful things we can offer to another in times of grief and loss is our presence. But it is not necessarily that easy. Anytime we help bear another's burden, we face our own fears and anxieties about the situation. Depending on the nature of what is happening—the context—we may be walking into rooms filled with emotion and raw pain, situations that can be difficult even for the most experienced servants. Without our bedrock faith in Christ, those fears may deter us. Without an understanding of Christ as the one who compels us to go to those in pain, we will never truly understand why we should go. That has to be first.

I love the scene in *The Bucket List* when Jack Nicholson's character, Edward, says he never knows what to say at funerals because he tries to avoid them. That's classic human avoidance behavior. Granted, it's fiction, but Edward has no deeper spiritual understanding of anything, therefore he is not about to walk into a situation that could be emotionally challenging. It's true; we avoid the things that bring us close to those facing death, and because we avoid them, we have no experience. Lack of experience breeds insecurity, and insecurity breeds words and behaviors that lack spiritual maturity or sensitivity.

Even when we have experience, those situations can still feel daunting and scary. It was no picnic trying to get ready to see Sarah in the hospital after the accident that severely injured her and killed her daughter. Unfortunately, most people stop right there and say,

"Well, that's going to be hard and very emotional. I won't know what to say and how to act, so I'd better not go." Out of fear, we do nothing. That is not the call of the church. While the rest of the world may run away from such pain or grief, that's when the church should be running in. We don't run away from it; we run toward it. Why? That's what Christ did for us. You can do it, even when you don't feel as though you can, because it is Christ who lives in you.

I'll never forget being in the kitchen of a home where a family had lost their teenage son. Teenagers and grief are always a tough mixture, so as the boy's friends gathered, many were obviously unsure of how to act around the parents and what to say to them. In the middle of all this activity, a young man came to the door carrying a plastic grocery sack with something in it. He walked up to the mother and said, "Mrs. Jones, I'm so sorry. Here, I brought you this." Holding out the bag for her to take, he then felt the need to explain, "It's Mountain Dew." The mother threw her arms around his neck and hugged him. It was such a simple act, but I had tears coming down my face over a two-liter bottle of Mountain Dew. While it was incredibly difficult to show up, this guy had chosen not to avoid the situation. He came, and his was a courageous, heartfelt offering that the mother will long remember. That's what the church needs to be doing.

Our call is to a faithful ministry of presence—a ministry that flows from what God has done for us. This is why it is important to make connections between our personal faith and theology; they will help equip us to serve others. God did not promise us that if we have strong faith and act obediently, he will keep us from pain. In fact, just the opposite is true. Look at these verses and notice the promise of presence.

> Do not be afraid; do not be discouraged, for the LORD your God will be with you wherever you go.
>
> Joshua 1:9

> Where can I go from your Spirit? Where can I flee from your presence?
>
> Psalm 139:7

I will be with you always.

Matthew 28:20 GNT

In this world you will have trouble. But take heart! I have overcome the world.

John 16:33

God promises us he will be with us. In times of death, our presence in the lives of others is a powerful incarnational ministry—a balm to hearts that grieve.

I'll never forget the day of my grandmother's funeral. It's difficult to put into words the depth of the impact she had on my life and childhood. I had just gotten out of the hospital following surgery for a collapsed lung when she collapsed and died of a heart attack at age ninety. Already exhausted, those next days were a whirlwind, especially since I was in Dallas, far from my home in Chattanooga. I went through all the rituals with my family, made it through the funeral, and finally we arrived at the cemetery. There were only a few of us there. It was cold. The wind was blowing. My face and my heart felt numb. As the minister concluded his words, we were each allowed to pick up a handful of dirt and throw it on the casket. It sounds like a simple thing, but until you have done it, you cannot imagine the magnitude and finality of such an act.

As I threw my handful down into the grave, I felt myself start to heave with sobs. I turned away from the grave and wound up facing the roadway, just in time to see my dear friend and mentor Bill Dudley getting out of his car. He had flown from Chattanooga to Dallas that morning, rented a car at the airport, gotten the cemetery location, and rushed to be with me, all without me ever knowing. When I saw him, it felt as though all the emotion I had been holding for so long let go. We embraced, and I sobbed for a good, long while. But here's the thing: we didn't speak. Words were not necessary. We started to talk only after we walked for a time. It was not the words that mattered. It was his presence.

It is always telling to me that people rarely remember what is said at funerals or memorials. They always ask for a CD or a recording so they can actually go back and listen to what was said. What they remember is who was there. They remember who came. Because I know how important it was for me that day, I have adopted the same model. Make no mistake, we bear one another's burdens best just by showing up. That's what the church should be about. Go. Be there. Show up for the visitation. Attend the funeral. Drop by the house. Make the effort. Whatever it is and however it can best fit into your life, do it.

What Not to Say

One of the things I often joke about with my colleagues is the wide variety of things you deal with in ministry that were never mentioned in any seminary class. No one teaches a pastor what to do when you accidentally throw the communion bread on the floor or what to do when someone asks you to do a burial for a body part that was found after the full burial had been conducted. In the same way, we all need practical counsel on the ins and outs of serving others in their grief. We can learn some of that from a book or a lecture, but we need to hear about the practical realities, the real-life situations that can occur, and how best to serve in them. I hope I can do that here, based on seeing others do it well—and not so well.

First, let's talk about words. As I discussed at the beginning of the chapter, there are things you should say and things you should not say. Along with the three phrases I mentioned at the beginning (God needed her or him; "I know how you feel"; the "angel" comment), here are a few others to stay away from:

1. *It's going to be okay.* At some point, that may be reassuring if you are a person who can actually help make it okay. I may say that to my wife or my child, but I would not say it to a friend who has just lost a loved one. It is not in my power to make it okay, and by saying it, I create the potential for hurt. The grieving person usually thinks, *How can you say that? You don't know that!* Again, you have to realize the

raw nature of emotion. Their world is shattered. It feels as if it will *never* be okay again; so any promise that it will be okay comes off as disingenuous at best.

2. *Call me if there's anything I can do.* People say that because they want to say something that makes them appear willing to help. I think it comes from a truly genuine place, but such a comment puts the onus on the grieving ones to make the contact. People in grief are most likely not functioning well. They are exhausted, and now you come along and give them something else they need to do. Don't tell them to call you. *You* put it on your calendar, and then *you* call *them.* When you are on your way to the grocery store, call and offer to pick up something for them. When you are out to dinner, call and offer to drop off something. When you are going to a movie, call and ask them to join you. Proactive kindness is far more comforting and helpful than saying, "Call me."

3. *How are you doing?* If you are in a quiet setting where the environment lends itself to actual deep sharing, then that question is fine. But if you run into someone at the mall or a ball game and with a concerned look ask how they are, it feels inappropriate and uncaring. The grieving person often thinks, *How can I possibly answer that question right now?* or, *How do you think I'm doing? For crying out loud, I just lost my loved one!* A far more appropriate thing to say is, "I've been thinking about you and praying for you." Merely acknowledging that it's not *business as usual* in that person's life is enough to move through such an encounter.

4. *It's God's will.* In the grand scheme of God's sovereign plan for the world, such a statement is true. God holds all matters of life and death is his hands, but saying it to a grieving person creates difficult emotions. This is where sensitivity to the stages of grief can be so important. Much like the "God picked a rose" comment, this can make the person feel instantly angry toward God. They are left to grapple with *Why would God will the death of my loved one?* or, *How do*

you know it's his will that I get a terminal illness? It creates very difficult questions in a very tender moment—questions that are best dealt with later in the grieving process.

What to Say

These words mainly involve sympathy or Scripture. Here are a few ways to comfort and encourage others:

1. *I'm so sorry.* It's hard to overestimate how helpful that phrase can be. It allows grieving people to know you identify with their suffering in some way. Most of the time, you don't need to say much more.

2. *I am faithfully, continually praying for you.* Reminding people that you are interceding on their behalf is a tremendous source of strength. As I have said before, this helps even more in the right environment.

3. *I sure do miss John.* A statement like this allows grieving people to talk about their loved one—something they desperately want to do. Naturally, this is something you can say after a few weeks or months have passed, and it highlights the value you place on their loved one's life and validates their feelings of loss. Too often we avoid bringing up the memory of the deceased as though that may make the other person feel bad. No! Bring it up! If we don't bring up his or her name, especially in the short term, it can feel to grieving people as though we have forgotten, as though no one remembers what they are going through. I often call people or stop them in a hallway and say, "I thought about you the other day when I saw this thing or heard that song, and it reminded me of Jerry."

4. *I do not pretend to know what you are going through, but I know the one who does, and I am asking him to comfort you in the hope of Easter morning.* Biblically grounded in the resurrection, it reminds them of the secure foundation on

which they stand. You would be surprised how often people start to feel as though they are out of control or losing it. A simple reminder of their core faith can be very reassuring. It also places you in the humble posture of not pretending to grasp the extent of their pain and potentially opens a door for them to share their pain with you in some way.

5. *I know this has been a hard journey, but remember that Joe has finally had his Easter morning.* This is something I have said to people over the years, and I mention it here because I am frequently told how comforting that statement was to them. The mental suggestion of Easter takes their mind off the physical and places it on the power of the resurrection. They instinctively picture their loved one rising with Jesus, or what that person may be doing in heaven, or what their loved one may look like in glory. All the earthly limitations—illness, struggle, pain, emotional distress, problems—are all gone, and the mental image of their loved one living in the freedom of new life is comforting in a most powerful way. The emotions surrounding death are strong, but the deep meaning of Easter to the Christian cannot be underestimated. Sometimes in the power of their emotions of grief and loss, people can lose sight of Easter. A simple reminder can be a comforting avenue for ministry.

When it comes to words, remember that they can be effectively shared in written form as well. In this age of technology, do not underestimate the power of a *handwritten note*. Because these days they're not the norm, they stand out. It suggests you went to an unusual amount of time and effort to communicate with them in a special way.

Another discipline that can be helpful is to *use your calendar* as a reminder to connect with the grieving person. I have a notebook calendar on my desk with one page for each day of the year. When someone has a significant event or loss I want to remember, I write it down on that date with the year. When I get to my office each day, the first thing I usually do is look at that particular day in my book, and depending on what's happened, I make an appropriate phone call or send a note. I also use my calendar in the immediate season following a death, making a recurring entry every three weeks to call or write the grieving person. Our lives move on quite quickly after we attend a memorial service or a visitation, but the lives of those who grieve continue with the aching void that sometimes feels more like an abyss. It can feel as though the world has moved on and forgotten. A timely phone call or note has the powerful ability to comfort and heal.

Ministry of Touch

One of the great blessings of Christian faith is the simple truth that God entered our physical, fallen world. God became like us in Jesus Christ and therefore knows what it is to feel. This is why I believe our ministry of touch is so vitally important. More and more there is scientific evidence suggesting that nonsexual touch has a powerful effect on us.

"Scientists are increasingly interested in the possibility that positive emotions can be good for your health. This study has reinforced research findings that support from a partner, in this case a hug from a loved one, can have beneficial effects on heart health," says Dr. Charmaine Griffiths, spokesperson for the British Heart Foundation.[2] I think we already knew that it's true, but it's all the better when we find that science agrees with us.

When Bill came to my grandmother's burial, the power of his embrace is what I remember. This is what others say to me as well. There is a man in our church who lost his nineteen-year-old son in a car accident, and when I went to his house the next day he said, "I don't remember what you said, but I remember you put both your arms around me and you hugged me in such a strong way." A widow who lost her husband when he was only sixty said, "Most of it was a blur, but I remember how tightly you held me." The power of the ministry of touch.

Obviously, this requires discretion. There are some people who do not like others in their physical space, and there are still others who do not welcome the embrace of those they do not know well. Even so, while it may not be a big hug, it may be a hand gently placed on a shoulder or a hand placed on top of their hand. Such acts lend depth and intimacy to ministry and echo the physical nature of God in Christ. We live in a physical world, and we relate to each other in tangible, physical ways.

This is especially important when it comes to one who is dying. The person often feels isolated or complains that no one touches him or her anymore. The only time the person is touched is by a nurse or a doctor, and often that touch is unpleasant in some fashion. It is natural for a visitor to feel anxious about touching a person who has cancer or who has tubes running in several directions or who has obvious bruising on the skin. Even so, you can usually find a place to make physical contact, ever so lightly. Ask permission to take the person's hand. If it's painful, he or she will decline—but at least make the effort. You may want to rest your hand on the individual's shoulder or arm and say, "Is this okay? I want to be sure not to cause you any pain or discomfort, so just let me know." Most of the time, he or she will be grateful that a caring human being expressed love in such a physical, tangible manner.

One of the most tender, heartfelt descriptions of grief and loss in all of Scripture is found in Acts 20. Paul is saying good-bye to the Ephesian elders, a group of leaders he had labored and served with in growing the church at Ephesus, leaders he had come to love deeply through the blessing of shared ministry and hardship in the name of Jesus. He is about to depart from his dear friends, every one of them knowing they will never see each other again. The grief borne in that moment of separation moves me every time I read it. Luke records in Acts 20:36–38, "When Paul had finished speaking, he knelt down with all of them and prayed. They all wept as they embraced him and kissed him. What grieved them most was his statement that they would never see his face again."

They wept. They embraced. They kissed. When appropriately offered, the ministry of touch incarnates the presence of Jesus. We wrap others in his loving arms. We become the touch of his gentle hand. It is the quiet affirmation that the grieving person is not alone in the world but instead is connected to others, and ultimately even to the larger community of faith.

In Difficult Circumstances

While every situation is difficult in some way, some circumstances can cast an even more challenging shadow on ministry, and thus, they are situations ripe for missteps and inappropriate words. These can be avoided if we give some thought to what we are doing before we actually enter the situation.

Suicide—Romans 5:20; 8:39

For a host of reasons I will not go into here, people tend to think of suicide as the *unforgivable sin*. I find that those who grieve a suicide victim often question whether that person is in heaven. Suicide is not the unforgivable sin, and if the person was a Christian, he or she is most definitely with the Lord. Yes, such an act appears selfish and is sinful, but it is not singled out in Scripture as somehow being worse than other sins that condemn us. The redeeming work of Christ is sufficient to cover even that transgression, and assuring those who grieve of that truth can be very comforting indeed. Paul's words in Romans 5:20 are particularly poignant at such times: "Where sin increased, grace increased all the more." You can't out-sin God's grace. Period.

There is also a certain shame that comes with the suicide of a loved one—shame that becomes attached to a family that is patently unfair. What we often fail to consider is the depth of emotional pain a person must feel to believe that ending his or her life is the best option. Further, the depth and darkness of emotional illness is something entirely unappreciated by those who have never felt it. Suggesting that a person who made such a decision was somehow a bad person or didn't love his or her family displays your ignorance. Resist such easy, worldly understandings and focus on the truth of God's Word. Romans 8:39 can also be helpful: "There is nothing in all creation that will ever be able to separate us from the love of God which is ours through Christ Jesus our Lord" (GNT).

Death of a Child—Matthew 18:2–3; 19:14

Never having been through this, I know I have no idea what it's like, and as we all do, I pray I never have to. I have walked with many families through such losses, however, and they are especially difficult because they fall into that category of being *untimely*. When someone dies before old age, we feel as though the person has been cheated; but when a child dies, that feeling is especially acute. As I have heard said many times, "Parents are not supposed to bury their children. It's supposed to be the other way."

Again, depending on the age of the child, parents may be anxious about their child's salvation. I always talk about the obvious, unique affection that Jesus has for children. In Matthew 19:14, Jesus says, "Let the little children come to me, and do not hinder them, for the kingdom of heaven belongs to such as these." And in Matthew 18:2–3, he calls a child to stand in front of the disciples and says, "Unless you change and become like little children, you will never enter the kingdom of heaven." Children are central to Jesus's teaching; he calls all of us to have childlike, sincere faith. Thus, we can affirm to those who grieve that Christ will be just that tender and gracious to the child they have lost.

Violence—Philippians 2:10; Revelation 20:11

When a person is murdered, not only does a family deal with the same issues related to an untimely death, but they also deal with questions of justice. There is a deep, natural human desire for the perpetrator to be found and punished. In the absence of that justice, grief can be all the more gut-wrenching. It also can become debilitating because it prevents the family from finding emotional closure.

In appropriate settings, it can be helpful to encourage people with the nature of God's character as one who is just. Part of God's holiness is justice, and the sins of this world will be answered. Philippians 2:10 reminds us that one day every knee will bow to Christ. All will answer to him. Revelation 20:11 describes the day of judgment. If Christ came to die for our salvation, then we know that God does not casually dismiss sin. It cannot be winked at or excused. It must be answered, and God will judge us according to our deeds. Therefore, in a world of vast injustice, the only way we can ever find peace, the only way we can ever sleep at night, is in the comfort of knowing that God is just. Injustice will not prevail, and we can comfort those who grieve with the hope of that truth.

Handling Your Own Emotions

The last thing I'll address on this topic is our need to handle our own emotions as we minister to others who are dying or grieving. I have suggested in several places that we need to prepare before we enter into others' lives to serve. Part of that preparation is anticipating some of the emotion we may feel, thinking through how we will react and what we can say, and reminding ourselves of the faith we profess. If we go to help bear people's burdens and then we go to pieces, we have not accomplished our task—we have only added to their burden. Our visit and our service should never be about us but rather about the people we're serving. As best we can, we need to steel ourselves to the raw emotion and agree internally that we will process it at another time. As I mentioned earlier, I have led many memorial services in which I preached and prayed and then after giving the benediction slid into a side room, closed the door, and wept.

Please understand that I am not suggesting you show no emotion. Tears and emotion are fine. Losing control of yourself, however, is not helpful. There is a difference between appropriate tears shared with the ones grieving and creating a scene in which others feel burdened to care for you.

A Sacred Privilege

Without question, our call to bear the burdens of others, especially in their grief or death, is a difficult one, but it is also a holy, sacred privilege. William Wordsworth wrote:

> There was a time when meadow, grove, and stream,
> The earth and every common sight,
> To me did seem
> Apparelled in celestial light,
> The glory and the freshness of a dream.
> It is not now as it hath been of yore;
> Turn wheresoe'er I may,
> By night or day,
> The things which I have seen I now can see no more.[3]

In other seasons of life, we see the meadow and the grove and the stream, but there will come times in our lives and in the lives of others when we can no longer see those things. Life no longer feels glorious. Instead, it's filled with grief and loss and pain and fear. Especially in those moments, just as Christ came to us, we are called to go to others, loving, serving, listening, and comforting with the incarnate presence of Jesus. May we appreciate that sacred privilege and know the presence of God's Holy Spirit as we go.

PART 2

The Journey
Continues

Getting from Here to There

4

How Do I Live with Loss?

Moving from Grief toward Growth

We do not want you to . . . grieve like the rest of mankind, who have no hope.

1 Thessalonians 4:13

Grief is exhausting and requires the strength of an Olympic athlete.

Barbara Ascher

Then suddenly, I am so angry. I am sick with fury, like a wounded animal.

Joyce Carol Oates, *A Widow's Story*

"It's amazing how everything can change in a single moment."

I did not know the woman who spoke those words, but she captured in a single sentence the deep shock and emotional numbness that had swept through the several thousand mourners gathered in my church. Her face was red and blotchy; you could tell she'd been crying for a while. Her eyes were not on me. Instead, she gazed at the scores of young people standing in clumps, arms intertwined, hugging, crying, hurting. Almost trancelike, she spoke more into the air than she did to me, almost as though her thoughts had formed words before she realized it.

Only days earlier a young couple, Laura Grant and Eddie Culberhouse, had been killed in a rollover car accident as they drove to the beach with friends. The accident happened on a Sunday morning, so our faith community was already gathered when the news began to spread. At first I could not figure it out. Moving from place to place I saw people gathered, some crying, obviously in serious conversation. It was highly unusual behavior for a Sunday morning. Finally, someone told me. Our church was heartsick.

In the days that followed, we quickly saw this tragedy had a far-reaching impact that went well beyond our church into our community. No matter where I turned, someone knew Laura or Eddie or was connected to them in some way. They had attended the same high school, and though separated by several years in age, each had embraced the other's group of friends. They were connected to several churches and youth ministries, fostering strong relationships in multiple groups that extended the positive reach of their lives. With few exceptions, I had not seen grief capture and hold a community quite like it did in this instance.

As a result, we knew the service would draw a large crowd. Both families agreed to a combined memorial service, and while that made the circumstances a bit more challenging, I worked hard to ensure that our campus would be ready and the service would be glorifying to God while celebrating their lives. What I had not anticipated, though probably should have, was how our community rallied around these two families. My phone kept ringing with offers of help from individuals, school administrators, youth pastors, and local companies—even from the NBA's Orlando Magic. Throughout our city, people of all ages and backgrounds were coping with the powerful nature of grief, desperately trying to find some way to help and assuage their pain. I'll always remember sitting in our sanctuary that day and looking out over all those people. In spite of their many differences, they were unified by their common loss.

I remember something the late Tim Hansel wrote in a book many years ago as he shared his experience of lifelong, chronic pain: "Pain is the common denominator of the human experience."[1] I certainly found that to be the case in my pastoral ministry. The pain of grief binds us all the more deeply. Grief, as odd as it may sound, creates community.

Still, everyone expressed their grief differently. Men sat silent and stoic. Teenagers unashamedly clung to one another. Mothers wept quietly. Others sobbed openly or tried to cope by organizing or giving directions.

Over the years as I have walked with the grieving and endured it myself, I've realized one thing to be a constant: no one ever grieves quite the same way as another. Laura and Eddie's memorial service provided a small glimpse of that reality. When you lose a person you love, no one hands you a textbook and says, "Just follow this guide and you'll be fine." It doesn't work that way. There's no formula. There's no right or wrong way. Sure, there will be common emotions and strategies, but even then, people will engage those at different times and with different emotions. And that's okay.

In the preceding chapter, I tried to give you some ideas about how to help others when they are grieving. In this chapter, I'm focusing on you. When you are the one grieving, how do you cope? How do you manage and sort through all the emotions, and how will that process change over time?

Some of you will be tempted to put this book down right now or move on to the next chapter. You may be in a season of grief and fear and think that reading this will only exacerbate your pain. Or maybe you aren't grieving, but you don't want to think about the possibility of something happening—what it may feel like when you lose someone you love. Both responses are valid, but let me encourage you to keep reading. If you are grieving, facing the depth of your pain is the only way you can begin to heal and move from the pain toward the life God has for you. And even if you are not presently grieving, walking around it and trying it on can be a very helpful exercise in your spiritual growth.

Simply put, grief is hard. It hurts. But Scripture reminds us that God doesn't want us to live there and put down roots. He wants us to keep moving. Psalm 66:10–12 provides a wonderful description of how God moves us through things. The psalmist describes a time of "burdens," "testing," and "refining," a time of going through "fire and water" (sounds an awful lot like grief to me). Thankfully, he does not stop there. He does not linger in his pain. There is movement, and that is the key element in this second part of the journey: we keep moving. The psalmist declares in verse 12, "But you [God] brought us into a place of abundance" —from grief to growth.

Certainly, when times get tough we can be tempted to give up and stop moving. This is the case for Elijah in 1 Kings 19. His circumstances are such that he tells the Lord, "Take my life" (v. 4). He's done, but God won't let him stop moving. God sends an angel with food to nourish him, and on the strength of that food (I believe both spiritual and physical food), Elijah travels another forty days and nights. He keeps going, and he fulfills God's plan for his life.

Moving from grief toward growth is never easy. It may well be the hardest steps you ever take. But examining your own feelings about the reality that awaits you, or that you are experiencing right now, is vitally important. Entering into that emotional place and temporarily *trying it on* helps prepare you for what will come. And knowing how God moves and strengthens you *in* your grief is a key ingredient in helping you keep moving. My hope is to shine some light on the darkness of grief to help you begin to see the next steps on your journey of faith in Jesus Christ.

A Lifelong Challenge

At its core, grief is the pain we feel from being separated from those we love, and like it or not, we deal with it our entire lives—from beginning to end. I'll never forget the arrival of our first child, John

David. My wife, Leigh, labored hard for twenty hours, but eventually the doctors discovered the umbilical cord was wrapped around his neck, so Leigh needed an emergency C-section. The sight of my son coming into the world is something that remains permanently etched in my mind. I was overwhelmed by joy, but needless to say, he was none too happy about it. As soon as the doctors cleared his airways, he started wailing and didn't stop. His little face contorted and turned a shade of red just like the horizon as the sun slowly sinks at dusk. He was flat-out angry. And who wouldn't be?

Up to that point, John David had a cushy life, living in the warm, nurturing environment of the womb where he had no needs or cares in the world. And then some stranger came and pulled him out of the only world he knew. The medical and scientific term for birth is *severed symbiosis*. We are literally severed from the symbiotic relationship we have with our birth mother, and we have been learning to cope with the pain of separation ever since. We don't like being separated from those we love and the things we value. When that happens, we grieve, and in our grief, we learn to cope. It's a core truth we seldom recognize or understand: *grief is only an earthly indicator of the ultimate separation we feel from the God who made us.*

Did you know that? From the time we entered this life, we have been struggling to come to terms with the deep longing we have to be reunited with our heavenly Father, the God who created us and planned for us from the foundations of the world. Because of our sin, we have been separated from him, and until we enter into the glory of heaven, we will never know the complete reconciliation for which our hearts yearn. Through Christ, we have a taste. In many ways, the kingdom of God *has* come, and we *are* in relationship with him. But one day, we will see and know his kingdom and the joy of our reunion with the Father in its fullness.

In the perfect plan of God's created order, however, he provides earthly relationships that fulfill us in this life, all the while pointing us to the greater hope of eternal union with him. Every human relationship we have is merely a taste of the intimacy and fulfillment we will know in heaven. Think about this: God made us relational beings because he is a relational God, both in his relationship with us and his own nature as Father, Son, and Holy Spirit. He uniquely created us, giving us the capacity to be in relationship with him. The earthly relationships we have are only finite expressions of what God yearns to enjoy with us eternally. And our lifelong yearning to be fully reunited with our Father is the deep, underground spring from which our earthly grief wells up. That's why our ability to cope with earthly grief is grounded in our faith in God through Christ. Thankfully, our grief has been answered in Jesus Christ, because through him our eternal relationship with the Father has been reconciled. Imperfectly now. Perfectly then. When we grieve, we can find comfort and hope in Christ's resurrection because through his sacrifice we are no longer *severed* from the Father by sin. Instead, we have the promise of eternal reconciliation with our Comforter.

Not Like Everyone Else

While many Scripture passages offer hope and comfort in grief, I want to look briefly at Paul's words in 1 Thessalonians. Along with Silas and Timothy, Paul founded the Christian church at Thessalonica. A great persecution erupted, however, and Paul was forced to flee for his life, leaving that community far sooner than he intended. From a spiritual maturity standpoint, the church was still in its infancy. Paul had yet to teach them many things. These young Christians were wrestling with questions about life, death, and heaven, and they needed Paul. He had yet to answer one of their most pressing questions: What happens at the end? So in chapter 4, Paul addresses some of those issues.

He writes in verse 13, "Brothers and sisters, we do not want you to be uninformed about those who sleep in death." In other words, there are things we can know about death, about those "who sleep in death." Did you hear that? God Almighty wants to inform us about the great mystery of death—this scary, veiled unknown we find so challenging to deal with. That's what I call good news! While we won't know everything about it, we can learn some things that will help and comfort us as we navigate our course through life.

We don't grieve like everyone else.

This is one of the first things we are told about death and dying. As Christians, our experience with grief will always be different from the rest of the world because our hope is in Christ through his resurrection. Paul says in 1 Thessalonians 4:13–14, "We do not want you to . . . grieve like the rest of mankind, who have no hope. For we believe that Jesus died and rose again, and so we believe that God will bring with Jesus those who have fallen asleep in him." And in John 16:20, Jesus says, "Truly, truly, I say to you, you will weep and lament, but the world will rejoice. You will be sorrowful, but your sorrow will turn to joy" (ESV). In Christ we view death differently through the lens of hope.

Conversely, the world grieves in the darkness of eternal death, believing that when this life is over, we're done. That's it. I remember standing by a locker at the YMCA in Chattanooga talking with one of my atheist friends. I asked him, "What do you think happens when you die?" He said, "Well, it's pretty much just nothing—forever." The other night, Leigh and I watched *The Descendants*, a movie that centers on the pending death of Alexandra King, wife of Matt King (played by George Clooney). When she finally dies, Alexandra is cremated, and the family sets out in a boat to inter her ashes in the water. When they finally reach the spot, Matt opens the jar, pours the ashes in the water, watches as they begin to sink, and says, "Well, I guess that's it." Then, to make it worse, the camera shot focuses on the ashes sinking to the ocean floor. The whole scene vividly illustrates the world's hopelessness when facing death without faith.

What's more, that hopeless grief is played out around us every day as people grieve, grasping at anything that may give them hope—things like angels or vague notions of reincarnation. They seek spiritualists who claim to speak to the dead. In my research for this book, I even came across an actual company called Afterlife

Telegrams that for ten dollars a word offers to deliver messages to the dead via terminally ill patients who promise to deliver the message once they pass into the next life. The fine print in their advertising says they cannot guarantee the message will get through because "no one knows what happens when someone dies."[2]

That's grief without hope. That's grief with desperation. That's grief grounded in fantasy that ultimately proves empty. Thankfully, God says we who are in Christ do not grieve like that. Faith in Christ is about the historical reality of the cross and the empty tomb. Faith is about being grounded in the eternal. Faith is about trusting in the Creator and Giver of life. Faith is about depending on the one who has defeated death. Hebrews 2:14–15 declares that Jesus "shared in their humanity so that by his death he might break the power of him who holds the power of death . . . and free those who all their lives were held in slavery by their fear of death." Thanks be to God, we are no longer slaves to death or our fear of death. Christ has defeated those foes, and so when we grieve it is with the hope of Easter.

To be clear, this does not mean the pain of grief is magically whisked away. Paul affirms in Romans 8:28, "And we know that in all things God works for the good of those who love him, who have been called according to his purpose." "All things" includes our losses and our grief. When we open ourselves to his Spirit, God can use even our grief for our good. As only he can, he will take our pain and draw us closer to him.

Grief is an acceptable Christian response to what we experience in life.

Paul does not say "don't grieve" or suggest in any way that grief is inappropriate or inconsistent with Christian discipleship. Just the opposite. He assumes that we *will* grieve but that we'll do it differently than the rest of the world. This may well be one of the most important things you need to hear: it's okay to grieve. You have God's permission. Let me say it again: *you have God's permission to grieve*. As odd as that may sound, it is often a truth we need to hear.

Several years ago, my assistant scheduled an appointment for me with a man in his midfifties. When he called, he indicated that he wanted to discuss some personal issues, so when we sat down, I asked some open-ended questions to give him the opportunity to tell me what was happening. Over the course of the next hour, he talked about his feelings of depression, his struggles in his relationship with his children, his unhappiness in his marriage, his dissatisfaction with his job, his poor physical health—the list seemed to go on and on. He had no sense of himself or any clear direction for his life. His relationship with God was distant at best.

Finally, I started asking a few more pointed questions about his family of origin, trying to find the basis for his feelings of worthlessness, when suddenly he started to cough—then choke—and then sob. His entire body was racked with grief and pain. He spoke no words, just buried his face in his hands and wailed—*wailed.*

I wasn't totally sure what to do next. I got up and put my hand on his shoulder. That one expression of comfort seemed to embolden him to continue. I put both my arms around him, his convulsions growing, and whispered repeatedly in his ear, "It's okay. It's okay. Let it go. Let it all out. Let it all out." Heaving, gut-wrenching sobs. Minutes passed, and then slowly, he calmed. Gathering himself, he looked at me and said, "My mother died fifteen years ago, and that's the first time I've ever let myself cry about it." He went on to describe his childhood and a poor relationship with his father that had blocked his ability to ever feel much emotion. For a variety of reasons, he never felt he had permission to feel those feelings and to grieve his mother's loss.

As it turned out, that bottled-up grief was the root cause of many of his other problems. Once he started to cope with the loss of his mother, the rest of his issues began to fall into place. The transformation of that man's life over the course of the next eighteen months was nothing short of amazing. All because he did a simple thing: in the context of a supportive Christian relationship, he gave himself permission to grieve.

And it's okay for you too. You can love the Lord deeply. You can have strong, solid faith. And you can also grieve. It's a normal, natural, and acceptable Christian response to the losses we experience in life.

Grief is not like the flu. It's not something you get over.

In all my studies on how Scripture discusses grief, I have yet to find a passage that says we ever get over it. Further, I have never met a single person who has looked me in the eye and said, "I'm over it." The only time Scripture discusses an end to grief is in Revelation 21:4 when John writes of the new heaven and the new earth: "There will be no more death or mourning or crying or pain." In heaven, we no longer will be separated from our Father. In heaven, death and grief are gone. While we live in this world, however, grief remains, and we never get over it. We may feel it less acutely. We may learn to manage it more effectively, but any expectation that we will one day say, "I'm over losing my dad," is a false idea.

Even so, we desperately want grief to be like the flu virus. We hope it'll finally go away. From time to time, people come to see me who have recently lost a loved one. Usually they say something like, "When will I get over this?" "How long am I going to feel this way?" or "It seems like it's taking a long time for me to get over this." It's difficult to look the person in the eye and say, "Honestly, you won't." I don't stop there, of course. I tell them it does get easier and that the pain will be less acute over time, but I stand firm that they will never get over it. There will always be a song, a smell, a movie, a holiday that brings our grief back to the surface. Like a dormant virus, it may lie quietly for extended periods only to stir and re-emerge once more. It is grief revisited, and it can be every bit as painful as when we first experienced it.

Coming to terms with that reality can help us move forward. If we liken grief to the flu, then we will continue to stay in bed, waiting until it passes to re-engage our life and our world. Knowing that grief does not pass, and honestly facing that reality, allows us to grow in our increased surrender and faithfulness. Grief becomes this new thing in our life that is our new normal. And like someone who learns to walk with a new knee, we learn to walk in the presence of this new stranger we would prefer not to know but which will remain with us nonetheless.

Our knowledge of the future gives us hope and strength in the present.

We know through Scripture that Jesus was acquainted with every grief we could possibly bear. Our experience with grief must begin with our deep understanding of Jesus's experience with grief. That is our common starting point.

The prophet Isaiah writes, "He had no beauty or majesty to attract us to him, nothing in his appearance that we should desire him. He was despised and rejected by mankind, a man of suffering, and familiar with pain [grief]" (Isa. 53:2–3). This truth buoys us in the knowledge that we are not alone. We grieve in the hope that Christ has already endured our grief. When we cry out, it's to a God who is deeply identified with the very thing we are presently enduring. We grieve knowing that while we do not get over it in this life, we will not endure it forever. It *does* have an end.

Knowing that is tremendously helpful. Think about it. If I'm at church in a boring meeting, I'll often look at my watch and imagine what I'll be doing when it's over. When I ran endless wind sprints as part of my training during my high school basketball days, I always told myself, *He can't make us do this forever*. The mere knowledge that my suffering would eventually end made my endurance of it at least somewhat easier.

As we learn to cope with our grief in this life, our knowledge of what is to come gives us strength. Sometimes we just need to remind ourselves of it. Imagining the return of Christ, the glory of heaven, or what life will be like in the fullness of time can bring a needed balm to the raw nature of our pain. Paul writes in Colossians 3:3–4, "Your life is now hidden with Christ in God. When Christ, who is your life, appears, then you also will appear with him in glory." Envisioning what those moments may be like keeps me going. What I'm experiencing now will not go on forever, so I forge ahead.

We grieve in different ways. There is no right or wrong way
or a correct length of time.

In the last chapter I mentioned the five stages of grief outlined by Elisabeth Kübler-Ross in *On Death and Dying* (denial, anger, bargaining, depression, acceptance). Too often we interpret those stages as if they are a road map. While they may give you some idea of what to expect, they are not linear or sequential. You will experience the various stages at different times and in different ways and to different degrees. You may be in three or four stages all at the same time or you may be in just one. Your unique process does not matter; you aren't being graded on how well you do. Don't get stuck in an intellectual analysis of how you are doing. Don't compare yourself to how others grieve or how your friend did. It's not a contest. The only thing that matters is that you are moving from grief toward growth, making some gradual movement, by the Holy Spirit. We can move forward through the stages because we do not grieve alone. Christ—the one who has already born what we now bear and emerged victorious—is always present. And that place of abundance will come.

From the common beginning point in Christ, how we each grieve will begin to diverge. As we do that, there are some helpful things to know that people have learned over the years. Perhaps simplifying Kübler-Ross's paradigm, many counseling manuals and other grief-related resource books talk about three phases or seasons of the grieving process: impact, recoil, and recovery. I prefer those words because they seem more descriptive of what I have witnessed in others, so let's consider them.

Impact

Physician T. E. Holt wrote a wonderful article for *Men's Health* magazine entitled "What We Learn from the Dying." I find it somewhat refreshing that a magazine normally focused on all things related to life and health would dare to discuss death. Dr. Holt describes his very first day of medical school. An anesthesiologist wrote three things on the board and had the class recite them:

Air goes in and out.

Blood goes round and round.

Oxygen is good.

"Keep those in mind and you'll be okay," he said. Then, he went over to the other side of the room and scrawled one word in big, black letters: DEATH. He said, "Stay away from this and you'll be okay." Holt said the class was somewhat unnerved by that, but the lecturer never erased the word. It remained there the rest of the class.[3]

How nice it would be if that were possible. If only we could make life that simple and matter of fact. Air. Blood. Oxygen. And, oh yeah—avoid death. Like a word written in bold letters, it seems to linger there in front of us. While we'd like to avoid it, we can't.

One day we will lose someone we love. We will get the news. Then what? That is the moment of *impact*. Denial, shock, disbelief, emotional numbness—all typical responses to the initial impact we experience. It reminds me of the disciples as they gathered following Jesus's death. They were in a locked room, gripped by fear. They were in shock at the reality of Jesus's death. Though Jesus had told them he would die, his death was now a reality, and they were trying to come to terms with what to do next.

In these moments of impact, I often marvel at how the human mind works. People who are dealing with the initial impact of loss often go into self-preservation mode. Emotionally, they feel almost detached from the experience, physically moving through what is necessary but not entering emotionally. I believe that is our mind's way of protecting us. We have too much to deal with too fast, so we shut it off, and then over time, we let small pieces of it in.

It's a bit like the story a counselor told me when I went for help with my own grieving. He said:

David, you are like someone who is trying to eat a one-hundred-pound block of cheese. You're trying to cram the whole thing down your throat at once. You can't do that. You're going to choke. The only way you ever make the block of cheese manageable is to faithfully and consistently carve off bite-sized pieces. Slowly, over time, you will turn that one-hundred-pound block into something that is far more manageable and easier to carry around.

The initial impact we experience in losing someone tends to feel like that one-hundred-pound block of cheese. It can be overwhelming. Don't try to pick up the whole thing. Don't try to deal with every single issue, every single piece of paper, every single phone call all at once. Take your time. Give yourself permission to do what you feel you are capable of doing on that day, knowing that more can be done tomorrow. Before long, you will find that you have accomplished a great deal, and you will gain confidence in the process.

The danger, of course, is failing to move out of the *impact* phase. A little self-preservation is fine, but if it extends for too long, then we impede our growth. I remember going to visit a widow on the second anniversary of her husband's death. When I arrived, she was very gracious. She offered me coffee and we began to chat. She seemed to be in very good spirits, and then she asked if she could show me something. I agreed, so she led me back to a room where she had carefully arranged all of her husband's things. His clothes, suits, shoes, recreational gear—all of it—was laid out and neatly arranged as if he were going to come walking in the door any minute. She spoke of her commitment to maintaining the entire room, almost as if it were a shrine. She was so proud of it, and yet it was a clear sign that she was not in a healthy place. Even after two years she had not allowed herself to move past numbness and denial. Prolonged self-preservation actually prevents us from moving forward. It keeps us from the growth God intends.

Corollary: Be careful in making major decisions. As I've said, we don't experience the stages or phases of grief sequentially, but I think it's important to make a note about decision making during seasons of intense grief. Obviously, you'll have initial decisions to make regarding funeral plans, burial arrangements, and the legalities of a person's will or closing a person's estate. I always recommend that you involve a pastor or trusted friend in these decisions and that you consult an attorney in matters related to the will or estate.

Once you get beyond those initial decisions, however, you'll be tempted to make major decisions too quickly, believing that radical change may assuage the grief or pain you feel. Rarely have I seen such snap decisions succeed. I think it is wise to wait *at least* twelve months before making any major life changes or adjustments. Allow yourself to get through the first year, to experience all the hard *firsts* that you will encounter—the first holiday, the first wedding anniversary, the first birthday, the first family event—the list of *firsts* can be long. The first year is an adventure in and of itself without adding the complications associated with major change.

Having navigated the first year, you will most likely have reached a place of enough emotional stability that you can make major decisions more successfully. If you decide you want to relocate after a year, then that may make sense. If you decide you want to take a major trip, then that may be what you need to do. But if you lose a loved one in January and decide to take a two-month safari to Africa in March, you may find yourself waking up in a tent, far from your systems of support, wondering why in the world you decided to do such a thing. Vacations are easily undone. Things like moving or changing jobs are not, so just a word of caution: be careful, slow, and calculated with major decisions.

Recoil

Once the initial impact recedes a bit, a person *recoils* or steps back to process and examine what has happened. During this process, a person begins to chart the way forward and deal with more of the emotional elements of grief: anger, anxiety, fear, guilt, loneliness, and sadness. I love Martha's honesty in John 11 when Jesus finally arrives to see about Lazarus. When she hears that Jesus is coming, she does not wait for him to get there. She runs down the road to meet him. I'm quite sure she wants to give him a piece of her mind. Lazarus has already died. Jesus had not made it in time, and she is angry. She says, "Lord . . . if you had been here, my brother would not have died" (John 11:21). In other words, "Why didn't you get here sooner? What took you so long?"

I wonder how many grieving people have uttered some variation of those words. We tend to feel as though God has let us down. Forgetting what God has already accomplished for us in Christ, we get mad at what we perceive as God's inactivity. *Lord, if you had just been here, if you had just shown up like I asked, then none of this would have happened.* Those are honest feelings, and we need to allow ourselves the space to feel them. We take a step back from the initial impact of grief and examine the many emotions churning inside us.

As such, in this season of stepping back or recoiling, it is also common for people to feel emotionally scattered. You're trying to cope with so many emotions all at once that you feel like you're all over the map. One woman said to me, "I feel so schizophrenic. One moment I'm a weeping mess and the next moment I'm laughing and telling a story. It's exhausting." And it is. (Yet another reason not to make major decisions too soon.) Give yourself a break. Grief ushers in a range of emotions; engaging each one is tiring. As simple as this may sound, you need more rest. Don't expect to have the same physical endurance you normally have. You have to take care of yourself. I've always liked how Anna Quindlen in her novel *Every Last One* provides a glimpse into the grief of a mother coping with the fresh, raw nature of grief:

> "I'm exhausted," I say to Alice, and I am. It is exhausting to pretend to be a different person for this length of time. Or not a different person—the same old person, who seems like someone I knew a long time ago. Mostly I have to do it in small doses—ten minutes here, an hour there. The rest of the time I busy myself with small repetitive tasks. I have thought about learning to knit, but I picture Alex leaving for school with misshapen sweaters and stuffing them guiltily to the back of his locker. Maybe I will make an afghan.[4]

Working through our emotions can wear us out, and it may often feel as though we are only an odd representation of who we used to be—someone we knew a very long time ago before this loss, this grief, entered in. So yes, we busy ourselves. We try new things. We cope. Some may knit. Others may pick up a new hobby. Others may join a book club or some other social outlet to foster new relationships. It's all different and it's all okay. We step back and feel the emotions. We grieve. We cope. We grow. We learn.

Depending on the situation, it is often healthy to seek the help of a pastor, a Stephen minister (specially trained lay minister), or a professional counselor to create the time and the environment to process your feelings. Unfortunately, too many people assume that if you just ignore your emotions they will eventually go away. They don't. Whatever we shove beneath the surface will find some way to get up and out, and that can often happen to our detriment. Don't ignore the feelings. Talk about them. Express them. Seek the Lord. Pray. Get counseling. All of these tools are important in moving toward growth.

Recovery

When loss first impacts our life, we struggle to deal with the raw emotions. We recoil a bit and begin to process more of our emotions and what our life may look like in the future. Then, unfolding through all that time, is our *recovery*. It is when we begin to move back into life with a new normal. It is not life as it once was, but it is the life God has for us nonetheless. As we trust in God's goodness and sovereignty, we attempt to embrace our next chapter. We start new routines. We start new traditions. Without really even being aware of it, we start spending more of our time looking forward than we do looking back. That's not to say we no longer feel lonely or anxious or angry at times. We do. The difference is that we are taking active steps to build a new life in the absence of our loved one.

Joyce Carol Oates wrote a poignant account of the sudden loss of her husband and her ensuing grief. As the book unfolds, you see her moving toward recovery, slowly opening herself to living life again. Her words mirror what I have seen in so many others as they walked the path of grief. She writes:

> When friends greet me with hugs, it's all I can do to keep from screaming and recoiling with pain . . . tears running down my cheeks even as I am smiling, smiling to assure my friends. "Yes, truly, I am feeling much better." Yes, truly, I *am* alive. For a while, there was some doubt![5]

In recovering from the loss of her husband, it was as though her improvement snuck up on her. Instead of mindlessly telling people, "I'm fine," she realized she actually was. Because those who grieve live in it every day, it is often hard for them to realize their progress. Parents who see their child every day do not realize their son or daughter's growth. But when relatives come to visit, they exclaim, "My goodness, Johnny has grown so much!" In the same way, we grow and recover through our grief, but sometimes it is so incremental that we cannot fully see it or appreciate it. But it's there. And God is there, ever faithful.

Grief can happen to us in different ways and at different times, but always at some point we'll think, *I actually* am *better. I'm still alive. God still has a purpose for me. I'll always grieve this loss, but it will not defeat me either.* Knowing that such a place exists can often give us the strength to keep going. Remember the words of Psalm 66:12, "You let people ride over our heads; we went through fire and water, but you brought us to a place of abundance." Believe this: such a place *does* exist. We may feel beaten down as though horses have just thundered over us, but there is that place of recovery.

In my moments of grief, when I feel as though the river is about to eclipse the top of my head, drowning me in my own sorrow, I try to envision the meadow on the other side. I think of the Lord's place of abundance. It may feel as though I am never going to get there. I may not be able to yet envision the steps I need to take, but the mere knowledge of its existence brings a strange peace to my soul. I picture myself walking there, feeling the warmth of the sun on my skin, smelling the faint scent of pine, and reveling once more in the wonder of being alive.

This description of death by Henry van Dyke has also helped me along the way:

> I am standing upon the seashore. A ship, at my side,
> spreads her white sails to the morning breeze and starts
> for the blue ocean. She is an object of beauty and strength.
> I stand and watch her until, at length, she hangs like a
>   speck
> of white cloud just where the sea and sky come to mingle
>   with each other.
>
> Then someone at my side says, "There, she is gone!"
>
> Gone where?
>
> Gone from my sight. That is all. She is just as large in
>   mast,
> hull and spar as she was when she left my side.
> And, she is just as able to bear her load of living freight to
>   her destined port.
>
> Her diminished size is in me—not in her.
> And, just at the moment when someone says, "There, she
>   is gone,"
> there are other eyes watching her coming, and other voices
> ready to take up the glad shout, "Here she comes!"
>
> "And that is dying."[6]

The hope and promise of our faith is that we *will* get there. We will make it to that glorious place of abundance where all our grief is caught up in the larger story of God's redemption. The challenge for us is living between now and then. As we each do that in our own unique way, let us remember that our grief is merely an indicator of our soul's deepest yearning to be reunited with our Father, the one from whom we have been separated since we drew our first breath. The deeper we go in our relationship with God through Christ, the greater our calm and comfort as we navigate the hardships and inevitable losses we endure.

5

How Will We Find Our Way Home?

Jesus Shows Us the Way

Oh, I have slipped the surly bonds of Earth . . . put out
my hand, and touched the face of God.

John Magee, *High Flight*

And if I go and prepare a place for you, I will come
back and take you to be with me that you also may be
where I am.

John 14:3

At the end of all our wanderings, we return to the place
of our very beginning, and see it, as if for the first time.

T. S. Eliot

Nothing pierces the heart of parents like the fearful cry of their
child. It can send shivers down the spine, and it certainly did for

me that day as I sat on my bed in a condominium on Jekyll Island, Georgia.

I was invited to speak at the annual Fun in the Son student conference, a summer gathering of roughly 1,500 high school students from all over the Southeast. The big blessing for us was that the conference leadership team always encouraged the speakers to bring their families. They believed this added authenticity and positive witness to the entire camp—and we were more than happy to oblige!

When we arrived that first day, we found that we were housed at the Villas, a large complex of condominiums and pools located right on the ocean. The units were built in clusters of ten to twelve units, and each unit looked almost exactly the same—same paint, same doors, same windows, same everything. The surrounding roads and landscaping also looked quite similar, so you had to pay careful attention to the letters and numbers on the building to be sure you were in the right place. Easy for adults—not so easy for small children.

Our particular unit shared a common pool with several other units in an open courtyard area, and that became our favorite spot. It was easy for Leigh and me to come and go—and with children who were five, four, and two, there was a lot of coming and going. Depending on who needed to be fed or who was napping, at least one or two Swansons were always on the move.

On our third afternoon, I was upstairs in our unit working on my talk for the evening. Kaylee was asleep in our portable crib, and Leigh had John David and Alex at the pool. That's when the adventure started. Our oldest, John David, decided he needed to go to the bathroom, so Leigh was left with a dilemma: pack up both boys and go in, or let John David go back by himself. From the pool to our condo was only about fifty yards, but it meant he had to walk between two buildings and around a corner to get to our front door. Leigh said, "Okay, John David, you can go by yourself. Dad is in the condo. Just walk down that sidewalk and around the building and you'll see our front door. We're in C106, okay? Look for C106." JD was thrilled by his newfound independence and happily took off.

The problem was that once he came around the corner, all the units looked the same, and in his excitement about being allowed to walk back by himself, he had forgotten the numbers. Not knowing what to do, he knocked on the first door he thought might be ours and got no answer. He picked another—no answer. He tried a third—no answer. At that point, he panicked. In his five-year-old brain, he was in a foreign land where apparently all the people had disappeared. He was desperately trying to get back home, but he did not know the way, so he just started screaming—and I mean screaming—my name: "DAADDDDDDYYYY!!!"

I heard it, though faintly. It was a long way off, but every parent knows the unique cry of their child. It was John David—and something was very, very wrong. I threw open the window and yelled, "John David? Where are you?" By then, he was completely frantic and yelled back, "Daddy, where are you?" I screamed, "Stay there. I'm coming!" I ran down the stairs and out the front door, only to find him one building over, nowhere near our unit. I ran to him. He ran to me. Hugs. Tears. I asked him, "Son, what happened?"

"I don't know, I just couldn't find home," he answered.

Home.

For most of us, that is a welcome, soothing word. Even for those who had a difficult childhood, home is still an ideal to be pursued, a reality yearned for and desired. Home is a place of security and safety. Home is familiar. Home is warm and loving and kind. Home is a place to be cherished and embraced. I remember in my early twenties when I suffered from debilitating panic attacks, the only place I ever found deep relief was the living room of my boyhood home. In that place there was no fear, no pain. It was home.

In our spiritual heart of hearts, that is the place we want to be, that place of absolute security, peace, and love. And from the moment of our entrance into this fallen world, we know this, don't we? Something deep inside tells us this can't be home, but that leaves us wondering: *If it's not, where is it, and how do I get there?* C. S. Lewis puts it well in *Mere Christianity*:

If I find in myself a desire which no experience in this world can satisfy, the most probable explanation is that I was made for another world. Probably earthly pleasures were never meant to satisfy it, but only to arouse it, to suggest the real thing. If that is so, I must take care, on the one hand, never to despise, or be unthankful for, these earthly blessings, and on the other, never to mistake them for the something else of which they are only a kind of copy, or echo, or mirage. I must keep alive in myself the desire for my true country, which I shall not find till after death; I must never let it get snowed under or turned aside; I must make it the main object of life to press on to that other country and help others do the same.[1]

We know this isn't our true country, but that journey to home raises many questions, doubts, and fears. My son went on a great adventure to find his way home, but he got lost—and scared. He was deeply afraid when he couldn't find his way, and that fear is common to us all. In that moment when death comes, will we know the way? I am reminded of Dante's words in *The Inferno*:

> Midway along the journey of our life
>   I woke to find myself in a dark wood,
>   For I had wandered off from the straight path.
>
> How hard it is to tell what it was like,
>   The wood of wilderness, savage and stubborn
>   (the thought of it brings back all of my old fears),
>
> A bitter place! Death could scarce be bitterer.[2]

Those words resonate with me. We know the feeling of waking up to find ourselves in a dark wood, savage and stubborn, the feeling of having wandered from the straight path. We're coming to the end. We believe in God, but the unknown seems overwhelming and threatening. Those fears grow all the more acute as we near the end of life or as we consider our mortality closely. We cannot escape the nagging sense that this is not where we were meant to live. We yearn to find freedom from the evil, sorrows, and indignities of this place, but how do we quell our fears and get back to the path that leads us from this life to the next, the path to our true home? How do we move from here to there?

These are spiritual truths that echo deep within us, and I find them emerging as people come close to death. Regardless of the circumstances of their lives, whether happy or sad, they want to know: How can I be sure I'll get home? How can I be sure I'll find my way to the Father? Please understand, it's not a sin to ask such questions or have such fears, even as Christians. Those fears only make us human. I do believe, however, that our journey toward everlasting life is a grand adventure, and God has given us the truth we need to quell our deepest fears. We can find peace and joy as we think about the end of our earthly life and our final journey home.

Trust Me; Believe Me

The good news for us is that we are not the first ones to go through this. We are not the first to feel that sense of fear and dread when considering our life's end. Look at the disciples in John 14. Jesus is sharing a meal with them, and what an eventful meal it is. He humbly washes their feet, turning customary practice on its ear. Next, he predicts that one of those seated at the table will betray him. The disciples are stunned and try to figure out who the betrayer may be. John 13:22 says they "stared at one another." Can you imagine what was going through their minds?

As if that's not enough, Jesus then tells them of his coming death. He says in John 13:33, "My children, I will be with you only a little longer. You will look for me, and just as I told the Jews, so I tell you now: Where I am going, you cannot come." *What?* The disciples must be thinking, *What do you mean we can't come? We've given our lives for you. Surely you are not going to leave us here alone!* You can almost feel the fear rising within them.

Obviously aware of their growing anxiety, Jesus gently comforts them. He provides them the truth that calms their fears, the same truth that has the power to calm our fears as well. He says in John 14:1, "Do not let your hearts be troubled. You believe [trust] in

God; believe also in me." I love that Jesus speaks so specifically to what the disciples are feeling. He can see their fear, so he says, "Wait a second. Hold on. Don't get upset. Don't be troubled by this. Trust me. Believe me."

The Power of Faith

Jesus emphasizes the importance of our faith and trust in God when dealing with our fears about the journey home. What a needed reminder. I don't know about you, but in my moments of fear I often forget the limitless, matchless nature of God. I forget the depth of his love and care for me. Instead, I see what appears dark and threatening and overwhelming. In the John 13 passage above, the disciples are totally focused on the prospect of Jesus's absence. They completely lose sight of all he has revealed to them in the prior three years. They forget he is the answer to their fears.

So it is when we come close to death. We forget. We forget Jesus has defeated death. We forget Jesus is our Resurrected Lord. As Fil Anderson, author, speaker, and longtime Young Life staffer, said on one of our staff retreats, we get *spiritual amnesia*. That is when we need the power of God's Word poured into us. That is when we need to reflect on the historicity of the empty tomb and Jesus's triumph over death. That is when we need to reflect on God's faithfulness and remember the one who is our Savior. That is when we need faith!

While we know the importance of faith; we also fear we won't have enough. I have spoken to numerous people who express that very fear about their death. We want to die well. We want to bear witness to our faith in Christ, but we worry that our faith will prove too weak. We worry we will lack courage. We worry our faith will not sufficiently sustain us as death approaches. Let's think about that for a moment. Who gives us faith? God does. We don't create faith. We aren't its author. God is.

Again, let's remember: Hebrews 12:2 tells us that Jesus is the author and perfecter of our faith. Romans 12:3 declares, "God has dealt to each one a measure of faith" (NKJV). If faith is given by God, will he provide it insufficiently? Never! Also, we don't actually need that much. Jesus says in Matthew 17:20, "Truly I tell you, if you have faith as small as a mustard seed, you can say to this mountain, 'Move from here to there,' and it will move. Nothing will be impossible for you." A mustard seed is a speck. Jesus says that when it comes to faith, you have enough to accomplish whatever is needed, including finding peace and security as you think about the journey home that awaits you.

Further, our faith is not in a road or a path. Sometimes we think finding the right road will lead us back home. If we want to get from New York to Miami, we take Interstate 95. Unfortunately, that is how some people approach their final journey home. *If I can just find the map or directions. . . . If I just follow the right road or observe the correct customs or perform the necessary tasks, that will get me home.* They think all they have to do is keep following that road, and eventually they will arrive. Not so.

Our way home is a person, not a path. Jesus says in John 14:6, "I am the way and the truth and the life. No one comes to the Father except through me." Our way home is not a series of actions or turns; it is a relationship with our heavenly Father, revealed in Jesus Christ.

John Bunyan's classic work, *Pilgrim's Progress*, illustrates this beautifully. As the main character, Christian, journeys toward the Celestial City, Formalist and Hypocrisy climb over a wall and join him on his way. He tries to explain to them that they can't just climb the wall and expect to get where they want to go. The journey is about the Master. They say to Christian, "What's it matter which way we get in; if we are in, we are in." Christian replies, "I walk by the rule of the Master, you walk by the rude working of your fancies. You are counted as thieves already by the Lord of the way, therefore I doubt that you will be found true men at the end of the way."[3] Stanley Fish, quoted in J. Ramsey Michael's commentary, points out, "For them, the 'way' is any way which finds them in an external conformity with the directions they have been given. They say to Christian, 'we are in the same *place* as you; are we not therefore in the same *way*?'"[4]

I know deciphering the elements of *Pilgrim's Progress* can be difficult, but here's the deal: The two intruders were on a road. Christian was in a relationship with the Master. They were in the same place but on a drastically different way. Jesus says in John 14:6, "No one comes to the Father except through me." Our faith is in the one we are with at the time our journey begins, and we only find the Father—we only get home—through him.

The Way Is the Cross

Granted, understanding how a relationship becomes our *way* can be difficult. The mechanics of our movement—getting from here to there—elude the finite mind. I remember a conversation with an elderly woman in hospice care. She said, "David, I have no fear about where I am going to wind up. I know where I'm going. It's getting there that scares me."

It's a question of transportation, which emerges as we try to apply physical realities to a spiritual world. Though movement in the spiritual world doesn't happen in the same way it does in the physical world, we still want to know. This transportation concept is often portrayed in the movies. In the 1970s film *Heaven Can Wait*, the newly deceased board an airplane at some sort of terminal in the clouds. Apparently, we *fly* to the Father! (I wonder if it's first class or coach.) In *Field of Dreams*, the deceased move from earth to heaven via a cornfield in Iowa, playing baseball as they go. In *Gladiator*, the main character enters heaven by walking through an old wooden door and then walking across a waist-high field of wheat. Even Elijah is described in 2 Kings 2:11 as going up to heaven "in a whirlwind."

In John 14, Thomas's mind seems to be in the same place as he wrestles with what Jesus has said. Thomas is thinking about roads, paths, and transportation. He says in John 14:5, "Lord, we don't know where you are going, so how can we know the way?" In other words, "We don't have enough information to plug into our GPS. How are we supposed to know which road to take?" I also love that he uses the term *we*. He is speaking for the disciples—and for all of us. We all want more details about this journey.

Thankfully, Jesus answers. Over and over again, Jesus answers, and we should rejoice. He does not want us in the dark; he wants us to know. He wants to quell our fears and provide comfort. In this instance, he answers with one of his many *I am* statements (Greek, *ego eimi*)—a statement that illuminates *how* he is the Way. Jesus makes it clear in John 14:6 that he is talking specifically about how a person can be *reconciled to the Father*. Scripture implies that *the Father* is the heart's true home. He is our destination. That's where we want to be—eternally. What Jesus reveals is that our destination is not actually a place but a person. (When John David was trying to find his *home*, he was actually looking for me. If home had been a place to him, there were plenty of condos to choose from. Home was only in the condo where I was.)

Jesus changes the entire conversation from roads, journeys, and destinations to the relationship between the Father and the Son—the relationship that enables us to find our *home*. When Jesus declares he is *the Way* to get to the Father, he is describing his unique and singular role as the Mediator between God and man. George Beasley-Murray, scholar and New Testament theologian, writes, "Each [*I am*] designation involves a mediation of humanity and the Father by Jesus: He is the mediator of the revelation of God . . . and of the salvation which is life in God."[5]

That salvation has come through one thing and one thing only: the cross. At the moment of Jesus's death, Matthew 27:51 declares, "The curtain of the temple was torn in two from top to bottom." The veil represented a very important element in Jewish tradition and history. It was the curtain in the temple that separated the Holy of Holies—the earthly dwelling place of God—from the rest of the temple where people lived and worked. No person could enter the Holy of Holies without risking death. But when Jesus's sacrifice was complete and death took him, the veil was torn. The curtain came down. The way to the Father was opened. Reconciliation with the Father had been accomplished. Further, the tearing of the veil was from top to bottom, indicating the movement was from heaven to earth, from God to humankind. The way was cleared at God's initiative, not ours. Salvation is his act and his alone.

Craig Barnes, former pastor of National Presbyterian Church and now president of Princeton Theological Seminary, writes:

> Our entrance into this household is based solely on the gracious activity of the Savior who brought us to his home with the Father, allowing us to leave behind the identity of nomads (or those who have no home) as we take our place in the pilgrim community that travels with God to God.[6]

We travel with God (Jesus) to God (the Father), and we do so through the work of the cross, which opens the way.

Our Companion on the Journey

In human terms, *how* we make the journey is hard to understand, but John 14 also reveals another comforting truth: we travel with Jesus. He is the Way, and he is with us the whole way. John 14:3 may be the most reassuring verse in the entire text. Jesus says, "I will come back and take you to be with me that you also may be where I am." We may not know the specifics of this journey, but we know one thing: Jesus comes and gets us, and then he takes us home. He is the Way. He is the means of our salvation. We get there through him with him. Just knowing that is enough.

For that reason I have always considered it a great privilege to be with a person when he or she passes from this life to the next. It is a moment filled with spiritual activity because it is the moment when Jesus comes. In a very real sense, when I am with a believer as he or she dies, I *know* Jesus is in the room. I've been in many spiritual situations, but I don't think I ever feel as close to Jesus as I do in these moments.

Whether it is a hospital room, a bedroom, the backseat of a car, or a battlefield, that space becomes holy, sacred ground, and *the person is not alone.*

I know many people struggle with deep feelings of guilt because they did not make it to be with their loved one as he or she died, or they worry endlessly about what their loved one went through because he or she died alone. Through the work of Jesus Christ, we can lay down those burdens. Hear this good news: *Jesus was there.* Allow the vision of Christ, strong and present with your loved one, to renew and restore your soul.

For the same reason, you don't need to fear you will die alone. Remember, at that moment, Jesus comes. He is your traveling companion on the journey. Heaven opens, and he takes you to be with the Father.

Sweet Reunion

As much as we hate separation, we love reunions. As I shared earlier, we all struggle with the pain of separation, the pain that comes from not being with the ones we love; however, we love the joy of reunions. I have two friends who do not live near me, and because of the circumstances of our lives and our families, we rarely see each other. That absence makes reunion so sweet, even if only for a short time. When I see either of them walking toward me, whether it's in an airport or a hotel lobby, words can't describe the joy I feel. It's felt in the embrace we share, the genuine nature of the look in their eyes. It is trust, love, grace, and affirmation all rolled up into a single moment. It is timeless, holy, and good. It's why families, high schools, and universities have been having reunions for as long as we can remember. We love them because in them we find joy.

Therein lies the comfort we yearn for as we face the prospect of our death. When Jesus comforts his disciples in John 14, he affirms that death is not so much about departure as it is about *reunion.* Yes, Jesus is leaving, but he's going to the Father. The Father and the Son will be reunited. Then Jesus will come get us, and he will take us to be where the Father is as well. We find our comfort in death by recognizing that it's not so much a departure as a joyous reunion with the Father.[7] Remember, God created us as relational beings. As such, every human relationship is but a taste and a promise of the fullness of our relationship with the Father eternally. Imagine the joy you feel when you are reunited with friends or loved ones you haven't seen in a long time; and now multiply that exponentially and eternally, and you still don't get close to the joy you will know when you experience reunion with the Father.

It's for that reason people often speak of being reunited with loved ones who have already died. Especially when someone has lost a spouse or a child, he or she will find comfort in facing death by anticipating a joyous reunion with that person on the other side. I say more about that in a later chapter on heaven, but that longing is simply a human expression of our heart's deepest longing to be reunited in the ultimate relationship we have with the Father. Our desire to see our loved ones is actually one more indicator of how deeply we long for the fullness of our relationship with God—the fullness of relationship that is complete and eternal. The human heart cannot conceive of such a thing in this life, but oh, how I look forward to that day.

Choosing the Right Lens

My sister is an ophthalmologist in Dallas. Once a year when I go home to visit family, she gives me a thorough eye exam, including a review of my current reading glasses. I can see fine at a distance, but I cannot see up close. Bit by bit, over the past five years, my vision has gotten worse. My sister says it's because my eyes are getting old, but I refuse to believe this. In any event, she gives me a new prescription—a new set of lenses through which I can look to read things up close. But here's the thing: I don't have to look through the lenses she prescribes. It's up to me. But not taking her advice would be foolish.

God, in his sovereign and gracious love for us, has given us the lens through which he wants us to see our coming journey home. I said this already in chapter 2, but it bears repeating: the lens is illuminated clearly in Psalm 121:1–2: "I lift up my eyes to the mountains—where does my help come from? My help comes from the LORD, the Maker of heaven and earth." As the psalmist thinks about the source of his help, he says he is going to be intentional about where he looks. He chooses to look up and not down. He is choosing to look to the Lord and not to the things of this world. He is using the lens provided for him by the hope of God.

As human beings, we live squarely in the middle of two realities: physical and spiritual. Because we cannot see or touch the spiritual, it is easy for us to focus on the physical. Especially when it comes to death and dying, we tend to linger longer on the deterioration of the body than we do on the restoration of the soul. We focus more on the physical life that is leaving than we do on the spiritual life being given. We are tempted to start seeing our death through the wrong lens. Paul is careful to remind us of this in 2 Corinthians 4:16–18:

> Though outwardly we are wasting away, yet inwardly we are being renewed day by day. For our light and momentary troubles are achieving for us an eternal glory that far outweighs them all. So we fix our eyes not on what is seen, but what is unseen, since what is seen is temporary, but what is unseen is eternal.

It is a question of perspective. As you consider your end-of-life questions and fears, what is your perspective? Where are you fixing your eyes? Physically, yes, we are aging day by day, but that is not the only reality. Paul reminds us that what we are experiencing physically doesn't even come close to the glory we will know on the other side. Let me encourage you to be *intentional*. I know the questions are not easy because they involve deep mysteries, but God has told us enough to overcome our fears. The challenge becomes whether we will choose to view our departure from this world through the lens of God's Word or through the lens of this world. Make the intentional choice the psalmist made. Look up, not down. Look at the great adventure before you through the lens of God's Word, and may you know his abiding peace as you trust in Jesus, your companion all the way home.

123

6

Why Not Go to Heaven Now?

The Significance of Life in This World

In the world's finale at the moment of eternal harmony God will bring to pass something so precious that it will suffice for all hearts for the comforting of all resentments, for the atonement of all the crimes . . . and make it possible to forgive.

Fyodor Dostoyevsky, *The Brothers Karamazov*

I have come that they may have life, and have it to the full.

John 10:10

If it is I who determine where God is to be found, then I shall always find a God who corresponds to me in some way.

Dietrich Bonhoeffer

"Wrongful birth."

The words grabbed my attention as I glanced at the newspaper headlines, waiting for my morning coffee to brew. The bold headline read, "Oregon Couple Wins 'Wrongful Birth' Lawsuit."[1] Wrongful birth? Before I could even read the article, I got stuck on the term. Was there such a thing? Well apparently in the state of Oregon there is.

The article described how a Portland area couple, Deborah and Ariel Levy, sued Legacy Health System for three million dollars because prenatal testing had failed to reveal their daughter's Down syndrome. During testing, tissue was mistakenly drawn from Mrs. Levy's placenta instead of the fetus, resulting in the incorrect results. The couple said they would have aborted their daughter, Kalanit, had they known she had the chromosomal disorder. Thus, the hospital system was guilty of a "wrongful birth." In other words, Kalanit Levy should never have been born.

The lawsuit was disturbing in its own right, but equally disturbing was the jury's response. Jurors deliberated less than six hours and returned a 12–0 verdict for the Levys, awarding them the three million dollars. Not a single juror dissented. The article even described how some jurors mouthed messages of encouragement to the couple as they left the courtroom following the verdict's announcement. The Levys insisted they were only suing for funds to help care for the special needs of their child, but their lawsuit created a firestorm of public debate. Is the life of a child with Down syndrome actually not worth living? Should the additional hardships of raising a child with Down syndrome be sufficient cause for parents to decline the privilege?

When I was a young pastor in Chattanooga, two families in our church had Down syndrome sons, and those boys became best friends. They grew up in the midst of the church family, became fixtures at church events, and lavished all who crossed their paths with love and affection. The impact of their lives on that congregation was immeasurable. Their families would have stated the exact opposite of the Levy lawsuit. A Down syndrome child may be more challenging to raise, but is that enough reason to declare that the child's life is a life not worth living? Hardly. Yet that seems to be where we have arrived. Quality of life or comfort in life now inform our view of what makes life worth living—a view that is often removed from God's design and plan for life.

As we explore our movement from this life to the next, the Levy lawsuit brings into sharp focus an important question. If, as I discussed in the first part of this book, our physical lives are filled with sin, death, grief, and pain, and if our promised everlasting life offers enormous hope and joy, then why not go ahead and go to heaven? Why invest and engage in the task of living this life fully when the next life appears to be so much better? Shouldn't we move there now? If we don't understand God's design for life in this world, then we may fail to fulfill the reason he put us here. Instead, contrary to God's will, we'll spend all our time yearning for heaven. The hope of heaven is vital to our present lives, but as the saying goes, you can be so heavenly minded you're no earthly good.

I have been asked about this dichotomy on frequent occasions. When I speak about death and dying and then describe the hope of heaven (more in the next chapter), people start to wonder. It would be like living in a slum and then having someone tell you there's a debt-free mansion waiting for you. Someone built it for you as a gift, and it's ready to move in to. What would keep you from rushing to the mansion? Answer: God has not finished his purpose for you in the slum. Compared to the glory of heaven that awaits us, this world *is* a slum, but God has infused our physical life with his divine purpose that centers on revealing himself, through Christ, as the hope of the world. Living this life to the full and to the glory of God is an enormous responsibility we hold in tension with the promise of immortality. In God's design, the latter cannot supersede the former. We must never see the living of this life as anything *lesser*. We were created according to the sovereign, perfect plan of God, and as long as we live, we must honor the Lord by faithfully serving him.

We also need to remember that the promise of heaven is not going anywhere. It's not like it has an expiration date on it. First Peter 1:3–5 reminds us:

In his great mercy he has given us new birth into a living hope through the resurrection of Jesus Christ from the dead, and into an inheritance that can never perish, spoil or fade. This inheritance is kept in heaven for you, who through faith are shielded by God's power.

We have been born, through Christ, into a hope that is alive in this world. We are shielded by God's power while we fulfill his calling on us here. So we have all we need for the living of this life. Also, our eternal inheritance—the riches of our everlasting life with the Father—cannot ever be taken from us. That inheritance never perishes, spoils, or fades. We can have absolute confidence that even as we live this life, the joy of the next one is absolutely secure.

In spite of that truth, the painful nature of life in this world can still create questions. A few months ago I visited a man who had recently lost his wife. She died at a relatively young age, and he was devastated. As I spoke to him about her promised resurrection and the glory she now enjoyed, I could almost see the wheels turning. He was in such pain. Life without her felt meaningless. Finally, he said, "David, I would just as soon go to heaven now to be with her. Why not? I don't want to live without her."

As hard as it is for us to comprehend at times, we do not live our lives for one person or one relationship. Instead, we live according to God's plan and purpose, and for his glory. It was her time. It was not his. God still had a design and purpose for his physical life before he enjoyed heaven. If the only thing we have to consider is how life works for *us*, then yes, we may start yearning to get out of *here* so we can get *there*. But that would be a fundamental misunderstanding of God's larger design for life and his design for our individual lives. It's a question of the purpose of life in this world, and that's what I want to explore in this chapter.

Cultural Influence

Over the years, we've seen several shifts in cultural views on end-of-life issues, and it's important for us to recognize historically how those changes have impacted our world. From the earliest moments of human history, life was lived in the context of community. The essential building block of society was the family unit, which was part of a larger system of families bound together in a particular area. The community was essential to everyone's survival. Whether it was hunting for or growing food, rearing children, or defending the community from outside threat, everyone understood his or her responsibility to the larger whole.

Those same communities also shared a common set of values. From the Middle Ages through the latter half of the eighteenth century especially, communities were governed by these shared values that flowed from a shared faith in God. Again, those values were essential for community survival. If you did anything to violate them and weaken the community, you were disciplined accordingly. The individual was always subordinate to the good of the community.

With industrialization came the explosion of urban population centers. A tectonic shift began to occur. More and more people moved to cities, and family life began to change. As family and community life changed, the shared faith and values changed with them. No longer was the foundation of the culture the family or community. The individual gradually assumed authority. In other words, each person was allowed to determine truth and was no longer subject to the truth of a larger whole. Consequently, truth became a subjective assessment.

As these changes gradually took root, several philosophical systems gained a foothold in modern thought. Let's look at three that widely impacted our shifting views about life and its purpose.

1. Postmodernism

In this system, worldviews are plural and relative. Absolute truth does not exist, and the way each person perceives the world is subjective. Each postmodern individual invents his or her own private moral world, his or her own self, his or her own values, and his or her own preferences that should be exempt from criticism, social norms, and moral laws. The standard defense of this private, individual world is, "I have values." But that is only partly true. Individuals may have values, but they are values only insofar as they benefit the individual in the sense of "I value it because I chose it and because it pleases me."[2]

Here's a good illustration that may simplify the influence of postmodernism: Three umpires are discussing calling balls and strikes in a baseball game. The first one says, "There are balls and strikes, and I call them *the way they are*" (objective truth). The second umpire says, "There are balls and strikes, and I call them *the way I see them*" (modernism or truth as personal interpretation). The third one says, "There are balls and strikes, and they aren't either *until I call them*" (postmodernism: truth is created for ourselves).

2. Objectivism

The idea of personal pleasure as a core pursuit flowed into the twentieth century through this philosophy championed by atheist Ayn Rand. This view holds that the proper moral purpose of one's life is the pursuit of personal happiness—a tenet that further fed the growing social shift toward individualism. People only have a moral obligation to themselves and their personal happiness—an approach that diminishes responsibility to their neighbor as well as any commitment to this life should they decide that living it no longer makes them happy.

3. Utilitarianism

As the definition of truth became increasingly determined by individual experience, and as individuals became increasingly focused on personal happiness, people began to have a more utilitarian view of life. Their values were determined by what worked or did not work for them. If the highest moral purpose for people is their own happiness, then they value what makes their lives work better. If something interferes with or complicates life, then they value it less. Subsequently, utilitarianism influenced the cultural view of life's value. That is, people will value your life *only* insofar as it benefits them. When it ceases to benefit them, they value it less.

These three philosophies unwittingly point us to a very dark place. When the individual becomes the sole authority in life, then meaning and purpose can be found only within ourselves. When we find no greater meaning or purpose in life than our own self-fulfillment, it is never enough to sustain us. Life collapses into a pointless, meaningless existence. The famous filmmaker Woody Allen was interviewed some years ago by *Esquire* magazine. At the time, Allen was being lauded for his creative genius and the unique nature of his films. By every earthly standard, he was enormously successful, but when asked about the impact of that success and his lasting legacy to film, he said:

> All man is left with is alienation, loneliness and emptiness verging on madness. The fundamental thing behind all motivation and all activity is the constant struggle against annihilation and death. You struggle to do a work of art that will last and then you realize that the universe itself is not going to last. Life is divided into the horrible and the miserable.[3]

While Allen's summations represent only a brief glance at these contemporary philosophical movements, I'll share a story that I think will help you connect the dots. Consider what took place on October 13, 2011, in the southern province of Guangdong, China. A van navigating a particularly narrow street in a crowded market area struck and then ran over a two-year-old girl. Surveillance cameras in the area showed the driver pause briefly, then drive away. They also showed the girl, grievously injured and writhing in pain, as no less than *eighteen people passed her by*. Then a second vehicle ran over her before a fifty-seven-year-old rag collector came to her aid. The very next day, October 14, 2011, a suicidal woman jumped into a lake near Hangzhou and began flailing helplessly. An American woman threw off her coat, jumped in and swam the sixty-five feet to the drowning woman and hauled her to shore. As others came to lend aid, the rescuer quietly slipped away without giving her name.[4]

The juxtaposition of those two events set off a wave of introspection in China, with many wondering what had become of their country. How could people walk by a dying toddler and lend no aid, and why did Chinese stand by until an American woman risked her life to save someone she did not know? Please understand that I am not making a sweeping generalization about the Chinese people or American people. The situation could have just as easily been reversed. The fact that it happened at all is the issue. It illustrates the vague indifference to life that has grown up in so many places—an indifference that threatens our culture in ways we do not fully understand.

How did those two situations unfold? No one reason can be given, but you can see the collective influence of varying cultural factors. Enormous numbers of people live in crowded urban centers with relatively little connection among them or any commitment to shared faith or values. Personal happiness and fulfillment are the determined priorities, so emotional investment in the needs of others is limited. Functionality and convenience are prized. A man hits a girl with his truck. What does he do? He hesitates, but he goes on. Why? He's working. He has other deliveries to make. Stopping would be a huge inconvenience to him and would require an emotional investment he is not willing to make, especially for someone he does not know. Radicalized individuality breeds radical indifference.

The next day, a woman jumps into a lake to save another woman who is trying to end her life. The expected response is indifference. If she chooses to die, then others should let her make that choice. It was not anyone else's concern. But another view of life emerges. A total stranger risks her life to save the drowning woman. It is a culture-rattling event, shaking the foundations of the masses and forcing them to reconsider their beliefs and their ideas about life. While I do not know whether she was a Christian, her actions reveal the heart of the gospel: love as sacrifice. Two moments. Two vastly different responses.

A Christian View of Life in This World

Given the hopelessness of life grounded only in self, Christian faith offers a joyous alternative. It calls us to life in a different kingdom with a different set of standards and shared values—a life infused with purpose. To the non-Christian, this view of life can be very hard to understand because it is not grounded in the standard values the culture champions. To a person who has no knowledge of the gospel, a worldview based on something outside the self feels foreign. In 1 Peter 4, Peter highlights this truth. He tells us in verse 2 that from the moment we come to Christ, we live our lives for God and for his purposes. Then he tells us that the rest of the world won't quite understand that choice. He writes in verse 4, "They think it strange that you do not run with them in the same flood of dissipation" (NKJV). When we live for God's kingdom instead of merely for ourselves, the world will not grasp why we are not plunging with them into all kinds of worldly behavior. Such life, to them, is a foreign concept.

Diognetus, a Roman scholar in the second century as Christianity was beginning to take root, once received an anonymous letter from someone trying to explain the phenomenon that he was witnessing in Christian people. The letter said:

> They live in their own countries, but only as aliens. They have a share in everything as citizens, and endure everything as foreigners. Every foreign land is their fatherland, and yet for them their fatherland is a foreign land. They marry, like everyone else, and they beget children, but they do not cast out their offspring. They share their board with each other, but not their marriage bed. . . . They busy themselves on earth, but their citizenship is in heaven. They obey the established laws, but in their own lives they go far beyond what the laws require. They love all men and by all men they are persecuted. . . . They are poor, and yet they make many rich; they are completely destitute, and yet they enjoy complete abundance. . . . To put it simply: What the soul is to the body, that is what Christians are in the world.[5]

We're different. And we're different because we have been called by God to live according to the example of Jesus Christ, a life of compassionate service and loving sacrifice. Our view of life radically differs from the rest of the world's, infusing everything we do with kingdom purpose while still holding before us the blessed promise of our everlasting life. Historian William McNeill wrote of Christian behavior during particular plagues in human history:

> Another advantage Christians enjoyed over pagans was that the teaching of their faith made life meaningful even amid sudden and surprising death. . . . Even a shattered remnant of survivors who had somehow made it through war or pestilence or both could find warm, immediate and healing consolation in the vision of a heavenly existence for those missing relatives and friends. . . . Christianity was, therefore, a system of thought and feeling thoroughly adapted to a time of troubles in which hardship, disease, and violent death commonly prevailed.[6]

Because we understand our immortality through Christ, we can live sacrificial, servant-minded lives committed to the greater good of building God's kingdom through the sharing of the Good News of the gospel. When others run away from the pains, sorrows, and hurts of this world, Christians run in because we understand this adversity is only a small part of the larger story of God's redeeming work. We have the hope of what is to come, but we also recognize the reason for which God placed us here: every life he made matters, and God desires to redeem each life. We become instruments in his hands to accomplish that larger purpose.

What's more, Christ came into this world to give us a rich, full, and abundant life. He doesn't say, "Do the best you can in this life because it really gets good for you in the next one." No, Jesus says, "I have come that [you] may have life, and have it to the full" (John 10:10). He did not come so we could just live but rather to give us a meaningful, joyous, and fulfilling experience. Obviously, not every experience will be a happy one, but Jesus tells us every experience is infused by God's greater plan and purpose. According to his sovereignty, he can use every moment of our life for his greater good. When we understand our life as part of God's larger purpose, everything we do matters. It is the abundant life of a disciple of Christ, a life infused with the joy of the Spirit of the living God because we are living our life for him.

Grounded in God's Nature

Our life view flows out of our core understanding of God's nature and character. God is our Creator. We believe that God has created everything in this life. That is where Scripture begins in Genesis 1:1: "In the beginning God created the heavens and the earth." John 1:3 declares, "Through him all things were made; without him nothing was made that has been made." The writers of Scripture were not historians or scientists, but they accurately explained the origins of creation. God was the Creator.

Further, what God created was good: "God saw all that he had made, and it was very good" (Gen. 1:31). If God is perfect and holy in his nature, then nothing could flow from his hand that was not also perfectly good. God created us *in his own image* (Gen. 1:27, italics mine). In a way that we cannot fully grasp as finite human beings, men and women reflect his image to the world. This truth is central to how we see ourselves and others. None of us were a mistake or an accident. None of us were a "wrongful birth." We were created by God. Our existence flows from the hand of the almighty God, and he has declared our existence good. When we earnestly reflect on the significance of what that means, we begin to sense some measure of the delight God takes in us. Zephaniah 3:17 says that God "will rejoice over you with singing." Think about it. God delights in us so much it makes him sing!

Not only do we gain confidence and security from the origins of our creation, but we also begin to see others the same way. We may not like every person in the world, but every person in the world was created by God. As such, each one bears his image even as we do. We cannot diminish the life of a single person, because each one was created by God and each life has been declared good. Each life has worth and value. Each life matters.

Let me also say that while everything God created is good, not every life is born in perfection, as any neonatal ICU unit will show you. We are born into a sinful, broken, fallen world. While we reflect God's image, we are all born with flaws and defects—some more noticeable than others. We are all born with unhealthy desires

135

that need to be surrendered to God's will and Word. That's why Jesus came, so that the sins that separate us from God will not ultimately prevail.

That truth brings us back to the question of our life's purpose. We were created to serve the living God, to glorify and honor him. It is the answer to the first question of the Westminster Larger Catechism: "What is the primary and highest purpose of human beings? As humans, our primary and highest purpose is to glorify God and enjoy him completely forever."[7] We were created for his glory and for the fulfillment of his purposes, not ours. Is there a promised, heavenly immortality awaiting us? Yes. But that future does not diminish the God-ordained purpose for which he made us, and we must always seek to live into that purpose. While contrary to the culture, that path leads us to the life we truly long for. We may not always understand the events and circumstances of our life or of those around us, but we can always trust in God's sovereign plan and purpose. We can take hope in the fact that there is a *reason* for our existence, and no matter what, God will be with us in it.

Some years ago, I was caring for a cancer patient in a hospital. The tumor was in his stomach and had metastasized to his liver and lungs, causing him to lapse into a coma. He lingered for days, his body physically wasting away. His continuing existence made no sense to me at all. Why did God allow this? Why not take him and end his suffering? Unbeknownst to me, this man had been estranged from his son for years. As I walked the floor one day, greeting and visiting as I normally did, I saw a younger man enter the dying man's room. When I walked in to offer support, I realized it was the dying man's estranged son. He was hunched over his father, sobbing. He began sharing with me the challenges of their relationship and his earnest desire to find peace with his father before he died. As we stood there, I encouraged him to talk to his dad.

Right there, the son began to pour out his heart to his father. The father could not react or respond, but something happened spiritually in those moments. We held his father's hands, and we prayed. By the time the son left, he had come to a place of peace and reconciliation with his father that he would never have known had God taken his father sooner. I cannot explain all the elements of what happened in that room, but I do know that even in the final, unconscious moments of that father's life, God had a divinely ordained purpose. He had a greater plan at work than just what I could see in front of me.

That's where we learn to trust our heavenly Father as we live this life. Too often we examine our circumstances and find no good reason for what's happening. Especially when we or one of our loved ones are suffering, we look to God and ask, "Why? Why are you allowing this pain?" In those moments, we want to take matters into our own hands. We want to reach up into heaven and pull God down to our level and say, "Well, because I can't come up with a good reason for why this is happening, there must not be one." Do you see the human arrogance in that attitude? In a sense, we're saying that God is no wiser than we are. We will beat ourselves to death by asking why.

If God is the omniscient and omnipotent God of all creation, is it possible he may have a plan at work that we are not privy to? Of course he does. And if God is holy and good and just, then while our finite minds may not be able to understand that plan, we depend on the fact that one day all things will be redeemed and made whole. We depend on God's truthworthiness and faithfulness—a fact that Scripture reminds us of over and over again (Deut. 7:9; 2 Sam. 22:26; Ps. 33:4; 1 Cor. 1:9; 10:13; 2 Tim. 2:13; Heb. 10:23; 1 John 1:9; Rev. 19:11).

Just as God promised, one day all things will be made whole. One day God will redeem every pain and every sorrow. Do you remember in John 14 when Thomas, the *doubting disciple*, feared he did not know the way to where Jesus was going? Later, even when news of Jesus's resurrection began to spread, Thomas did not believe it. He insisted he would not believe until he touched the wounds in Jesus's side. Jesus gave him that chance when he appeared again and said, "Put your finger here; see my hands. Reach out your hand and put it into my side. Stop doubting and believe" (John 20:27). Here's what I want you to see: Jesus was glorified, but the wounds were not gone. *His wounds became part of his larger glory.* We sometimes think that when we get to heaven, all our wounds will disappear and be forgotten. Not so. Based on what I see in this Scripture passage, I don't think that's it. I think our wounds—the painful nature of our life's experience—make heaven all the more sweet.

Let me explain: If you had a dog you loved that was a huge part of your life and you lost that dog, you would be devastated. You would do everything you could to find it. Now imagine how you would feel when after a number of days, even when all hope to find him seemed lost, you found your beloved dog. In some mysterious way, you love your dog all the more in that moment. And you feel that way *precisely because* you had the experience of losing him. The pain of having lost him is taken up in the greater joy of getting him back. That's what I'm talking about. Our wounds become part of the greater joy of heaven. Just as Jesus's wounds were taken up into the larger story of his resurrection, so ours will be as well. In the holy mystery of God, the wounds and pains of this life will make our everlasting life all the more joyous and sweet. Wow.

Fyodor Dostoyevsky said it well in his famous novel *The Brothers Karamazov*:

> I believe that suffering will be healed and made up for, that all the humiliating absurdity of human contradictions will vanish like a pitiful mirage—the despicable fabrication of the impotent and infinitely small mind of man. That in the world's finale, at the moment of eternal harmony God will bring to pass something so precious that it will suffice *for all hearts for the comforting of all resentments, for the atonement of all the crimes of humanity, of all the blood they've shed and that it will make it not only possible to forgive, but to justify all that has happened with men.*[8]

Through Christ, at that moment of eternal harmony with God, something precious indeed will happen. All that has happened in this life will be redeemed, and our redemption will be made all the sweeter by the sufferings we have borne here.

Living in the Tension

In the end, our understanding of life's value will be determined by our faith in God and the truth God has communicated to us in and through Jesus Christ. Over the last 150 years our culture has eroded the faith foundations and shared values on which our society was created, and we have replaced them with a radical individualism that denies the absolute truth revealed in God's Word. The individual is now the authority. Each individual person now determines what is true for him or her, and that determination is based on personal happiness, utility, and convenience. Out of that worldview comes a diminished view of life—one that can quickly rob us of God's design and plan.

When Dietrich Bonhoeffer was wrestling with the rise of Nazi Germany in the mid-1930s, he was faced with some of these same questions. How could one race of people make the determination that another race or class was not as valuable and thus not worthy of living? In a letter Bonhoeffer wrote to his brother Rudiger in 1936, he openly shared his thoughts:

> If it is I who determine where God is to be found, then I shall always find a God who corresponds to me in some way, who is obliging, who is connected with my own nature. But if God determines where he is to be found, then it will be in a place which is not immediately pleasing to my nature and which is not at all congenial to me. This place is the Cross of Christ. And whoever would find him must go to the foot of the Cross, as the Sermon on the Mount commands. This is not according to our nature at all, it is entirely contrary to it. But this is the message of the Bible.[9]

Sadly, we have moved as a culture into the place Bonhoeffer described, a place where God always corresponds to what we think and what we want. Out of that, we can be falsely led toward giving up on this life to more earnestly pursue the next—and the joy of immortality. Our anticipated everlasting life informs our present life, yes. That knowledge blesses and gives us hope and strength, but it should never cause us to believe our lives are just about us. They are not. Our lives were created by God for God.

As Bonhoeffer says, we can essentially create God in our image instead of the other way around. If our relationship with God is truly personal and real, then God must have the power to contradict us, to tell us things we don't know and do not want to hear. If we acknowledge God as the Author of truth and Creator of all life, then God will determine where he is to be found, and that will not always correspond to our whims and desires. Our relationship with him is about so much more than our personal pleasure or happiness or about finding places that are congenial to us. It is about nothing less than the salvation of the world and building God's kingdom. When we put life in that context and acknowledge that all life flows from the hand of our holy, almighty God, then we will live in the proper tension between this life and the next. We will live in the confidence, purpose, and humble responsibility of being God's instruments in this world, while at the same time anticipating and rejoicing in the wonder of our future home—our immortality with God. We will move from this life to the next. We will know the joy of everlasting life through Christ, but that is always given to us in God's time and in view of God's overall design and purpose for life.

PART 3

The Journey Concludes

The Joy of Our Eternal Home

7

What Is Heaven Like?

Life in Our Father's House

Shed not for her the bitter tear, nor give the heart to
vain regret;
'Tis but the casket that lies here, the gem that filled it
sparkles yet.

from the gravestone of Sarah Starr,
August 19, 1830, to December 28, 1877,
great-great-great-grandmother
of my wife, Leigh Swanson

We have a building from God, an eternal house in
heaven, not built by human hands.

2 Corinthians 5:1

Ready.

That's how I thought he looked. Billy Graham looked ready.

How I wound up seated across from him on a private plane is
something only God could orchestrate. It was April 1995 and I had

spent the last few months trying to care for Lane Newsom, a dear friend who was battling an aggressive malignancy. We spoke on the phone often, and Lane had asked me to teach her how to pray. As her faith began to take hold, I asked her if she would like me to come to Dallas and hold a small prayer service for her healing. She agreed, so I invited Reid Henson, a good friend and elder at Signal Mountain Presbyterian Church, to join me.

Reid had been healed from cancer on two separate occasions and had a powerful healing ministry to cancer patients all across the country. As an executive with the Coca-Cola Company, he had access to their fleet of planes, so he reserved a jet for our trip. This was something I had never done in my entire life—fly on a private plane! Two days before our scheduled departure, our nation endured a great tragedy when the Alfred P. Murrah Federal Building in Oklahoma City was bombed by terrorists Timothy McVeigh and Terry Nichols. The lives lost totaled 168, including sixteen children. Our nation went into collective mourning.

As community and national leaders made plans for a public memorial service, Dr. Graham was invited as the primary preacher. He accepted the invitation even though he was not in particularly good health at the time. Hoping to avoid commercial airline travel, Dr. Graham's staff contacted friends at Coca-Cola, inquiring about use of their Atlanta-based private jet. It had been checked out to Mr. Henson, so they approached him about changing his plans to accommodate Dr. Graham. Late on the night before our trip, Reid called me and said, "David, we may have a slight change in plans. How do you feel about flying from Chattanooga to Asheville tomorrow to pick up Dr. and Mrs. Billy Graham so we can fly them to Oklahoma City? Then we will fly on to Dallas and come home later that night."

Needless to say, I was ecstatic. Spending time with one of the great Christian leaders of our time was a gift too large to comprehend, and the actual experience did not disappoint. I sat across from Billy Graham the entire trip—three hours of listening to stories about his ministry and asking him every question I could think of. He even showed me his manuscript for the sermon he would give the next day in Oklahoma City. It was an amazing time—at least until we started to land.

As we were getting ready to make our initial descent into the Oklahoma City area, a line of thunderstorms came up out of nowhere, stretching from west Texas through southeast Kentucky. We could all see the radar screen, and the line of storms was filled with reds and purples. The pilot informed us there was no way to fly around it, so we would be descending through it, which would not be pleasant. We all turned our chairs to face the front of the plane, buckled our seat belts, and braced ourselves. In the twenty minutes that followed, I endured the most jarring, hair-raising experience I have ever had on an airplane. It felt as though we were a pinball, bouncing all over the sky, ascending and descending in sudden, rapid bursts. I clutched the armrests of my seat, knuckles white with fear, sweat rolling down my back.

Then at one point I turned to look at Dr. Graham seated one row behind me across the aisle. I could hardly believe what I saw. His legs were comfortably crossed, right over left, with his chair slightly turned so he could get a better view out the window. His right arm was folded across his waist while his left elbow was braced on the armrest, his chin resting in his left hand with not the slightest hint of tension in his body. He looked like he was listening to a symphony or a concert. As I looked at his face, it occurred to me: he was not the least bit concerned about what was happening to that airplane because either way, he was ready.

His gaze out the window suggested he knew something the rest of us didn't. He knew for certain what Paul told the Philippian church: "For to me, to live is Christ and to die is gain" (Phil. 1:21). In fact, it was Billy Graham who had made the evangelistic question famous: "If you were to die tonight, do you know for sure that you would go to heaven?" Judging from the look on his face, he was sure! Years later, after the passing of his wife, Ruth, the words he wrote confirmed my thoughts: "The death of the righteous is not to be feared—it is not to be shunned. It is the shadowed threshold to the palace of God."[1] As I stared at him that day, plane bouncing hither and yon, I imagine he was dreaming of what it would be like to finally inhabit the palace of God. My fear revealed that I lacked such perspective, and I have tried to learn and grow from that moment ever since.

Interestingly, in a recent survey by *Christianity Today*, 46 percent of Americans said they never consider the question "Do you know where you would go if you die?"; 11 percent said it occurs to them about once a year.[2] Perhaps they do not think about it because there is so little known about what happens after this life. Or because they think heaven is only a fairy tale or part of lore or legend. Nothing could be further from the truth. Yet surprisingly, 85 percent of Americans believe in heaven—that somehow life does not end at the grave.[3] God has not told us everything about heaven, but he has revealed an enormous amount through his Word. As we understand those truths, we can come to a different perspective on this life, gained through the knowledge of what is yet to come.

Heaven Is Real

In trying to understand heaven, we must first acknowledge that we contend with the cultural images that bombard us every day, many of which present heaven as either a fairy tale or a fictitious idea. These cultural images are more fiction than fact, and we can be lulled into a sense that heaven is a psychological creation of a needy human mind rather than a real place. Scripture makes it clear that heaven is far more than an idea. It exists. It is not a hoped-for reality but an ongoing spiritual home for the living God and those who have come to him by faith.

John paints this picture beautifully in Revelation 21:10–21. As the book begins, John is taken up into heaven in a mysterious fashion. It is hard to say exactly what happened other than it was a dramatic spiritual time for him in which God revealed specific, glorious things that he instructed John to write down. In Revelation 1:19, God commanded, "Write, therefore, what you have seen." Clearly, what God revealed to John was something he wants us to know. In Revelation 4, John saw an open door and then heard God's voice say, "'Come up here, and I will show you what must take place.' . . . At once I was in the Spirit, and there before me was a throne in heaven" (Rev. 4:1–2). In God's mystery and power, he brought John to a view of heaven. Some of the things revealed there are hard to understand, but some are not. Some are simply majestic, hopeful, glorious pictures of what awaits us.

As always, God tries to explain a heavenly reality in terms we can understand. Jesus does this as well. He often says, "The kingdom of God is like . . ." and then paints a verbal picture. To say the description John writes in Revelation is exactly as heaven is can be a bit shortsighted. As finite human beings, there is no way we can possibly understand the limitless wonder of heaven. As Psalm 139:6 declares, "Such knowledge is . . . too lofty for me to attain." But God does paint a picture for us that allows us to grasp important truths. In fact, he goes to great lengths in Revelation 21 to describe heaven's proportions so that, as much as is humanly possible, we can understand the wonder that awaits us.

For us, it is like buying a home and then describing it to our best friend. It may or may not be a literal description, but that does not change the truth that John is communicating: *heaven is a real place, and it is glorious in every one of its perfect dimensions.* John describes heaven as being 12,000 stadia in each direction—width, depth, and height. Anne Graham Lotz, Billy Graham's daughter, spoke on this at the Christian Life Conference at Montreat, North Carolina, in 2000.[4] She worked with a map and surmised that if you plot those dimensions, it is a 1,500-square-mile cube—stretching roughly from Mexico to the Canadian border, from the Rockies to the Atlantic Ocean, and then again that high.

To give you an idea of the size of that, if you had 20 billion residents, far more than the population of the world today, each person would have seventy-five acres. John is saying that heaven is vast, expansive, and there is room for everyone.

Then John describes the walls: they are more than 200 feet thick and made of jasper—a stone with diamond-like qualities. The point is that such a wall is impenetrable. No enemy can get through it.

Ultimate security. The foundation of the city is twelve layers, each made of a precious stone. In other words, the foundation is solid. It will not shift or crack. The gates are pearls. The streets are gold. I hope you're getting the picture. God reveals heaven to John in such a way that he can describe it in very specific terms that reinforce its reality. It is completely safe and secure, and its foundation is rock solid. It will never fold or collapse. Does that sound like an idea or a fairy tale to you? Of course not. God has revealed what we need to know in order to be secure that heaven most definitely exists. Heaven is a real place.

Our Father's House

Finite minds will always find it hard to grasp infinite truths, but God has made another truth perfectly clear about heaven: not only is it real, but it is where he lives. It is his home. He lives in a place not made or soiled by human hands. In John 14:2, Jesus says, "My Father's house has many rooms." As he appeases the disciples' fears about his departure, he begins to explain to them that he is going to heaven—to his Father's house. The most beloved of all the psalms, Psalm 23 concludes with, "Surely goodness and mercy shall follow me all the days of my life, and I shall dwell in the house of the LORD forever" (ESV). David is making a clear reference to the life that is to come, affirming that it will be lived in heaven—"the house of the LORD." As those transformed by the redeeming work of Christ, that house will be our future dwelling place.

With that truth as our foundation, we keep building. Because heaven is where God lives, we can make certain assumptions about what heaven will be like. We will be living in a place where we will know all the fullness of God, the fullness of his nature. Paul writes in 1 Corinthians 13:12, "Now we see only a [poor] reflection as in a mirror; then we shall see face to face. Now I know in part; then I shall know fully, even as I am fully known." Right now we know only a part of the fullness of God's nature. We know a part of his love, a part of his peace, a part of his joy. Paul tells us, however, that *then*—in that time when we enter everlasting life—we will know him fully. We will see God, in all his glory, face-to-face.

Take a moment and imagine that. Think of all that God is, and then imagine living in the fullness of that being and the fullness of that nature—all the time. Heaven is the fullness of God's love, his peace, his joy, his hope, his grace, his wisdom, his power, and his mercy—and you will experience all those things at the same time, all the time. Finite minds cannot conceive of it. It is far too grand and glorious to even comprehend. When we begin to internalize this amazing truth, how can we not find comfort and hope in this life through our contemplation and anticipation of the life that is to come? This is also what I think of when I hear people say they fear heaven may be boring. Can you imagine being bored in the midst of all that? Hardly!

We must consider the opposite truths as well. Heaven will also be the absence of all that God is not. Heaven is the total absence of hate and the complete absence of sorrow. It is the complete absence of grief and chaos and disappointment and fear and depression and sadness and self-loathing and confusion. None of that exists in heaven. Shortly after seminary when I was dealing with a particularly painful loss, Laurel Neal, one of my beloved classmates, sent me a poem that she always held dear in such times. Written by Jane Kenyon, "Notes from the Other Side" captures well the hope of heaven. In heaven, she writes, we are divested of sadness, of daily irritations and wastefulness, of poverty and illness. "Our calm hearts strike only the hour, and God, as promised, proves to be mercy clothed in light."[5]

Heaven is that marvelous place where we divest ourselves of all that God is not, and we live eternally in the presence of all that he is. As one who has known the pain of dropping a clod of earth on the casket of a loved one, I find Kenyon's description especially hopeful.

Note that if we say that heaven is a real place, then we must also affirm that hell is a real place. While this is not a book, or a chapter, on that reality, it must be said. If only those who are in Christ are received into heaven, then there is also a place where those who reject Christ are exiled. If heaven is the fullness of all that God is—love, joy, peace, hope, mercy—then hell is the fullness of the absence of all those things. Hell is the complete absence of love. Hell is the complete absence of peace—and joy, hope, and mercy—and everything else that is of God. God does not dwell in hell, so all those things are gone. Conversely, hell is the fullness of what God is not. Hell is the fullness of chaos and evil and sadness and grief and darkness and anger and malice. Make no mistake, there is judgment, and if God's wrath has not been mitigated for us in Christ, the outcome is not good. Hebrews 10:30–31 is a sobering reminder: "'The Lord will judge his people.' It is a dreadful thing to fall into the hands of the living God." Revelation 20:15 states, "If anyone's name was not found written in the book of life, he was thrown into the lake of fire" (ESV). There are other Scriptures that affirm this too (see Matt. 5:29–30; 25:41–46; Jude 7, 13), but this will suffice for my purposes here.

All Things Revealed

As a pastor, I get a lot of questions, many of which start with the word *why*. It is a common desire for human beings to want to understand what is happening to them in this life. It is not enough for us to experience something, good or bad. We want to know *why* it happened. We want the reason. If we have faith in God, we believe the reason can be traced back to him, so we go to him for that answer. What I often say in response is that this side of heaven, we don't get the answer; "I'm going to ask him when I get there." There are things that God is doing in this life that we simply cannot see or know, purposes we are not privy to. That's why Paul says, "Now we see only a [poor] reflection as in a mirror" (1 Cor. 13:12). We just don't see well here.

In heaven, however, we will see *very* well. In the same verse Paul says, "then we shall *see* face to face" (italics mine). In Revelation 21, when John receives that glorious vision of the heavenly realms, he writes, "I saw" (v. 2). And in verse 23 we learn one reason why we will see clearly: "The city does not need the sun or the moon to shine on it, for the glory of God gives it light." In other words, there is no darkness in heaven. The glory of God lights up the place. While things in this world seem dark and filled with shadows, heaven needs only the light of God's glory. All things are seen and known.

When we come to live in our Father's house, all the *why* questions get answered. Everything will be known to us. Heaven is perfect clarity. All things are crystal clear. What's more, you will not have to pull out your list of questions to ask God why certain things happened during your life. Answers to those questions will be simply known. Nothing is hidden. Nothing remains in the shadows. Revelation 22 illuminates this for us. John writes, "Then the angel showed me the river of the water of life, as clear as crystal, flowing from the throne of God and of the Lamb" (v. 1). Again, all things are clear—seen—revealed. Then in verses 4–5, John continues: "They will see his face. . . . There will be no more night. They will not need the light of a lamp or the light of the sun, for the Lord God will give them light. And they will reign for ever and ever."

In heaven there is no darkness because God illuminates all. Again, nothing is in the shadows. Nothing is hidden. All is seen and known. Can you imagine what that will be like? I imagine it will be a little like the euphoria you get when you finally understand a math problem or work out a puzzle or solve a complex situation at work. For a time there is no answer, but when the answer emerges, you feel tremendous satisfaction. Multiply that exponentially, and it still does not come close to what heaven will be like. Consider all the time and energy you invest in trying to understand things in this life, trying to work out or solve complex issues or situations. When you arrive in heaven, those days are over for good. You will see. You will know. You will understand. Why? Because you are in the eternal presence of the Light of Life.

Horatio Spafford believed in spite of his grief when his four daughters were lost at sea when their ship, the *Ville du Havre*, sank in 1873. Traveling to England to meet his wife, he wrote the words to the beloved hymn "It Is Well with My Soul" at almost the same spot where the ship was lost. The famous last verse reveals how

Spafford was comforted in the coming *sight* that will one day be found in heaven:

> And Lord, haste the day when my faith shall be sight,
> The clouds be rolled back as a scroll;
> The trump shall resound and the Lord shall descend,
> Even so, it is well with my soul.[6]

One day, faith does become sight. One day in heaven, all things will be known. Even in our deepest fears and pains, we can say with Spafford, "It is well with my soul."

The Joy of Reunion

Our anticipation of heaven is fueled by the prospect that one day we will know and understand all things. But don't forget about the further joy of seeing all the other people gathered there. Heaven is always described as a place inhabited by a lot of people. We aren't going to be living in the middle of eternal nowhere. Far from it. We will be in the midst of all those who have gone before us by faith. And we'll know them. In the perfection of heaven, we will completely know one another. I alluded to *reunion* in chapter 5, and I want to explore that idea more fully here.

As hard as that is to grasp, we will know everyone there, even those we did not know on earth. And we will most especially know those we loved here. Scripturally, this is revealed most clearly in that sacred moment on the Mount of Transfiguration recorded in Luke 9:28–36. Jesus takes Peter, James, and John up to a mountain to pray, and as he prays, he is transformed into glory. Two men appear with Jesus and speak with him. Peter is overwhelmed by it, and in a bid to stay, he offers to make tents. Jesus has made no introductions, yet Peter says, "Master, it is good for us to be here. Let us put up three shelters—one for you, one for Moses and one for Elijah" (Luke 9:33). In the mystery of God's glory, Peter knew these two men. He had never met them before, never seen their faces, yet in their glorified form, he knew them. And so shall we.

We'll know our spouse. We'll know our children, those who were born into this world and those who were lost prior to their actual birth. We'll know our parents. We'll know our friends. And we'll know the heavenly host whom we never met while on this planet but who are part of the one family of God through Jesus Christ.

Luke 14:15 describes the kingdom of God as a great banquet, a moment when we will all sit down together at the great feast of God. I imagine heaven in that way, all gathered around one table, all in the presence of the living God, all things having been reconciled to himself; and we will know those around the table with us. I have often heard the question asked, "What is your fantasy dinner party? If you could have dinner with anyone, living or dead, who would you pick?" Well in heaven that becomes reality. We have dinner with everyone we'd like to know, even those we never knew in this life. Venerable Bede, a church historian in 710, put it this way:

> A great multitude of dear ones is there expecting us; a vast and mighty crowd of parents, brothers, and children, secure now of their own safety, anxious yet for our salvation, long that we may come to their right and embrace them, to that joy which will be common to us and to them, to that pleasure expected by our fellow servants as well as ourselves, to that full and perpetual felicity.[7]

As good as that sounds, we also need to realize that our relationships will not have the same value to us as they do now. In this life, every human relationship is a placeholder for the perfection of what will be our reconciled relationship with God in heaven. When we finally enter into that joyous reunion with God, all other relationships will be usurped by the joy of the one we have with him.

Although they won't diminish our singular focus on God and our worship of him, we will still take delight in the relationships we have with each other. God made us as relational beings. Part of the joy of our existence is in the relationships we share with one another and the delight we find therein. Simply because we will not need those relationships in the same way does not mean we will not enjoy them. In his book *Heaven*, author Randy Alcorn writes,

Christ is heaven's center of gravity, but we don't diminish his importance by enjoying natural wonders, angels, or people. On the contrary, we'll exalt him and draw closer to him as we enjoy all he created. Deep and satisfying relationships will be among God's greatest gifts.[8]

Further, we will also know reconciliation with all those gathered there. Paul writes in Colossians 1:19–20, "For God was pleased to have all his fullness dwell in him, and through him to reconcile to himself all things, whether things on earth or things in heaven, by making peace through his blood, shed on the cross." In heaven, all things will be reconciled to God. All wrongs will have been righted. Peace will define our experience. Just as the angels announced at the birth of Christ, "On earth peace, goodwill toward men" (Luke 2:14 NKJV), peace will ultimately be completed in heaven. We will have only goodwill toward one another.

Perhaps the best earthly representation I have ever seen of this heavenly reconciliation comes from the 1984 movie *Places in the Heart*. It's the story of a white widow in 1935 Waxahachie, Texas, who tries to save her family farm. The movie vividly portrays the brokenness of human relationships: the widow still aching with grief; the husband who has an affair and wrecks his marriage; the drunken black boy who accidentally shoots and kills a white sheriff; the KKK who capture the boy and drag his dead body around town. The end of the movie, however, offers a picture of heaven, though I didn't realize it initially. The camera closes in on several characters at a church service having communion. But as the camera pulls back, all the characters in the movie are there. The unfaithful husband passes the tray to his wife. The white widow passes the tray to the husband she lost so early in life. Finally, the black boy passes the tray to the sheriff he killed and says, "Peace of God."

I find it quite odd that in this life people who deeply and genuinely love the Lord cannot figure out how to live together in peace. Our inability to do that is further evidence of the insidious nature of sin. But I am buoyed in the knowledge that such brokenness will not last. When we all arrive in heaven, I will turn to those I have been separated from in this life, and we will know the healing reconciliation of God, granted to us in and through the shed blood of Christ. We will pass the trays to each other, and all will be made whole again. All the things that have separated us as people, all the things that have torn societies and cultures apart, all the things that have brought bloodshed, violence, and hatred will disappear.

In heaven there is no such thing as racism or classism. There are no political parties or denominations. (I think I may find the absence of denominations one of heaven's greatest blessings, given how much of my life I have devoted to issues within those systems.) There are no private clubs. Death is gone, and so is divorce. There is no ageism or sexism. The corruptions of human sexuality are all made whole. There is no such thing as abuse or neglect or emotional manipulation. There are no countries or states or nationalities. Every barrier, every obstacle that has ever separated human beings from one another, they all come down through Christ when we reach the shores of heaven. Can you imagine such a place? Can you imagine never having to worry about what others think of you or what someone has said about you? Can you imagine never worrying that someone will take advantage of you or feeling awkward as you enter a place by yourself? Imagine perfect unity and relationship with everyone all the time. That's heaven.

Suffering Removed

When we move into our immortal state and take up residence in the heavenly realms, all suffering will end. I think this may well be what people look forward to the most, because we all know what it is to suffer, and to suffer acutely. God promises us that we will have trouble in this world, but he also says he has overcome the world (John 16:33). He tells us that if the world hated him, it will also hate us (John 15:18). This world is a hard place to live in, but heaven is the opposite of that. Revelation 21:4 reminds us, "He will wipe every tear from their eyes. There will be no more death or mourning or crying or pain, for the old order of things has passed away." The old way of the world—living with suffering and evil—is gone.

In heaven mourning and grief are nonexistent because death does not exist. All tears are wiped from our eyes because there is nothing and no one left to wound us. We are no longer separated from our loved ones. There is no more crying, no more pain, no more physical illness or limitation. Cancer is done—over. Chemotherapy never again has to be endured. There is no more heart disease or heart attacks. No more autism or Down syndrome. No more diabetes or Crohn's disease or diverticulitis. No more depression or anxiety or schizophrenia or bipolar disorder. No more hunger, thirst, or famine. There is no more poverty.

In the glory of heaven, it's all over and done with because Christ took all that suffering and pain on himself at the cross. I think it's an important point for us to consider here. As I mentioned earlier, 85 percent of Americans believe in heaven, but relatively few consider the question about whether they will go there when they die. I find that so odd. Scripture makes it plain that you don't go to heaven unless you are in Christ, redeemed by his blood. It is a thought often left out in our greeting-card world. Songwriter Julie Gold writes in a song about heaven, "I think I'll go to heaven, there I will lay me down."[9]

I love the song, but the sentiment is wrong. You can't just say, "I think I'll go." It's more than that. You go only if you are accompanied by the one who opened the way. George Matheson put it this way in his hymn "O Love That Will Not Let Me Go":

> O Cross that liftest up my head,
> I dare not ask to fly from thee;
> I lay in dust life's glory dead,
> and from the ground there blossoms red
> Life that shall endless be.[10]

The ground of heaven blossoms red from the blood-stained ground of the cross, granting us an eternal inheritance far beyond what we can ever imagine. Our suffering is gone because his suffering has been offered on our behalf. It is only by his blood that we ever enter therein, which is why God's call on our life to share the Good News is so vitally important. The lives of many hang in the balance today, and they will never know the glorious hope of heaven unless we share Jesus with them.

Do We Go to Heaven as Soon as We Die?

We often want to apply human constructs to God, trying to make physical realities apply in what will be a spiritual world. When we die, we cease to exist in human time and space. In heaven, we exist in an *eternal now*. There is no concept of time as we know it. So any concept of *waiting* is nullified. So the answer is yes. As soon as we die, we go to heaven. Chapter 32 of the Westminster Confession of Faith puts it this way:

> The bodies of men, after death, return to dust, and see corruption: but their souls, which neither die nor sleep, having an immortal subsistence, immediately return to God who gave them: the souls of the righteous, being then made perfect in holiness, are received into the highest heavens, where they behold the face of God, in light and glory, waiting for the full redemption of their bodies.[11]

A few Scriptures inform us as well:

> The dust returns to the ground it came from, and the spirit returns to God who gave it.
>
> Ecclesiastes 12:7

> He [the criminal on a cross] said, "Jesus, remember me when you come into your kingdom." Jesus answered him, "Truly I tell you, today you will be with me in paradise."
>
> Luke 23:42–43

> We are confident, I say, and would prefer to be away from the body and at home with the Lord.
>
> 2 Corinthians 5:8

In addition, Luke 16:22–31 depicts the beggar Lazarus in heaven and the rich man in hell immediately after they die. There is no waiting.

From these texts, we can discern that when we die our spirits leave our bodies and immediately join God in heaven. There is no delay, and there is no intermediate step, such as the Roman Catholic view of a place called purgatory. Christ's sacrifice is sufficient for the redemption of our sins. We don't need to fear that we may not utter a last prayer of confession prior to death or that we are somehow not righteous enough to enter heaven right away. Jesus said on the cross, "It is finished" (John 19:30). The work of justification has been done. Our sins have been paid for, and we will arrive in heaven as the sons and daughters of the living God, redeemed by the blood of the Lamb.

Why This Changes Us

In closing this chapter, I want to emphasize the significance of heaven in our day-to-day struggles. Too often we think of heaven as a hoped-for future, the place we will eventually get to but not something that can make a difference in our here and now. To the contrary, what we believe about heaven has enormous significance for us today. Jewish psychiatrist Victor Frankl, arrested and imprisoned by the Nazis in World War II, wrote a book called *Man's Search for Meaning*, in which he discussed the manner in which human beings deal with suffering. He described, sometimes in disturbing detail, the way his fellow prisoners coped with the hardship of their lives. Some gave up, yet others managed to survive even though they were stripped of every shred of human dignity.

He wrote, "There is nothing in the world . . . that would so effectively help one to survive even the worst conditions as the knowledge that there is a meaning in one's life. . . . In the words of Nietzsche: 'He who has a *why* to live for can bear almost any *how*.'"[12] The *why* for Christians is the fulfilling of the plan of God's ultimate kingdom and the knowledge that one day we will inhabit that place in all its eternal fullness. Frankl's point is that our ability to endure suffering is far greater when we have hope. Why do you suppose America puts so much emphasis on the *weekend*? For many, it is the means by which they endure the hardships of the workweek because they have the hope of the weekend. The week will end, and they will finally be able to relieve their stress. Well, heaven is the ultimate end of that psychological coping mechanism. Heaven is the ultimate answer to the things we suffer, because when we have faith that our suffering will be relieved and one day end, we can endure. We can persevere.

This is life-changing good news. Heaven, and our contemplation of it, keeps us going. In my ministry there are times when I run into the hard questions I have mentioned in previous chapters.

Why is a little girl killed in a car accident when she was belted in?

Why does a young man die of a brain tumor just after his first child is born?

Why does a mother die in childbirth?

Why is a baby stillborn?

Why do humans treat each other with such dishonesty and cruelty?

People frequently ask me how I cope with the enormity of the issues I deal with every day. At least one of the ways I cope comes from my reflections on heaven. I know these questions and issues and evils do not last. I know that one day all things will be known. I know that one day I will no longer stress over how to comfort these families and friends. This truth is absolutely critical for me in my personal life and ministry. Without heaven, these questions and events would crush me.

One of the first challenges I faced when coming to First Presbyterian Church, Orlando, was the sudden death of one of our college students, Barrett Burchak. He was a student at Florida State University and was killed on the Florida Turnpike while coming home one weekend. His parents, Andy and Cary, have since become close friends, and I'll never forget the way they welcomed me, a new yet strange pastor, into their home during a time of such grief. Three years after Barrett's death, Cary wrote me this email:

One thing facing such loss has revealed to me is the reminder that this is not our home. While I am called to live a life "here" that brings glory to the Lord, my eyes and my heart look toward eternity a little differently now. There is new meaning to Jesus's words, "Lay up for yourselves treasure in heaven."

The hope of heaven transformed the way she understood her circumstances, including the loss of her son. This hope allowed her to find the resolve to persevere and to live a life that honors and glorifies the Lord. She does it beautifully.

This life is only for a season, and then all things shall be known. I know that one day, in the joy of heaven, my tears will be dabbed, my wounds will be healed, my relationships will be reconciled, and my burdens will be lifted—forever. Knowing that brings me such hope that I rise each day fully aware of the presence of God and the calling of God, not yet in their fullness, but sufficient for the life I live in this world.

One of my favorite books of all time is J. R. R. Tolkien's *The Lord of the Rings*, usually published as three books. It is an epic tale that pits the forces of good against the forces of evil, and it is made all the more endearing by the fact that a tiny little man, a hobbit named Frodo, endures the greatest suffering and carries the greatest responsibility in vanquishing evil forever. As you know, the books were made into movies, and toward the end of the third film, *The Return of the King*, one of Frodo's hobbit compatriots, Pippin, and the great wizard, Gandalf, have a conversation about what is to come as one epic battle appears to be lost.

With the enemy armies approaching, Pippin says, "I didn't think it would end this way."

"End?" Gandalf replies. "No, the journey does not end here. Death is just another path, one that we all must take. The grey rain curtain of this world rolls back and all turns to silver glass . . . and then you see it."

"What, Gandalf? See what?" Pippin asks.

Gandalf, ever gentle, replies, "White shores . . . and beyond. . . . A far green country under a swift sunrise."

"Well, that isn't so bad," Pippin remarks.

"No . . . No it isn't." Gandalf smiles.[13]

Over the centuries, humans have characterized heaven in various ways, with most of those images depicting a peaceful, joyous place. Scripture points us to more than an image. As we think about our immortality and our movement from this life to the next, we stand on God's truths. Yes, death is a path we all must take. But the white shores and the beauty of the far green country Gandalf describes are enough to help us endure the battles of this life. When we think about it—when we take the time to actually reflect on it—we realize heaven is more than just *not bad*. It's the place where our Father dwells in all his fullness, the place where all things are brought to unity and completion in the perfect harmony of God, the place where I will finally fully understand, and the place where I will dwell in the unending, unfathomable nature of his love. I don't know about you, but I can't wait to get there.

8

What Happens in the End?

Why the New Heaven and the New Earth Matter

If you read history, you will find that the Christians who did most for the present world were just those who thought most of the next.

C. S. Lewis, *Mere Christianity*

Then I saw a new heaven and a new earth, for the first heaven and the first earth had passed away, and the sea was no more.

Revelation 21:1 ESV

The new heavens and the new earth ought to set the trajectory of a Christian's life so profoundly that his life doesn't quite add up when the world looks at it.

Kevin DeYoung and Greg Gilbert,
What Is the Mission of the Church?

Several years ago Orlando had one of its bigger moments when the Amway Center opened. Home to the Orlando Magic NBA franchise, the new arena is the centerpiece of a major redevelopment in what had been one of the city's more economically depressed areas. It was also intended to symbolize the team's commitment to winning while keeping their megastar, Dwight Howard, happy. (Obviously, that did not happen.)

As the arena rose up from the ground over a two-year period, the anticipation grew. Season ticket sales soared. New restaurants and retail shops opened. Stories ran regularly in the local paper touting the entertainment features to be offered, the huge electronic scoreboard, and all the technological improvements over the former arena. They even published the number of men's and women's bathrooms. You get the picture—Orlando was jazzed about this new arena.

Several months before the grand opening, arena officials and Magic administrators strategically heightened the buzz by taking community leaders on special group tours. Lucky for me, I got an invitation to one. Given all the excitement, I was thrilled to get a behind-the-scenes look at what all the hype was about, and I must say, it did not disappoint.

I won't bore you with all the details, but suffice it to say, the arena was, and is, phenomenal. We started the tour on the ground floor, the centerpiece of which was a huge Orlando Magic gift shop. We went up floor by floor, seeing administrative offices, locker rooms, catering and kitchen facilities—you name it. Finally, the elevator doors opened on the main level. We all stepped out, and it was like a sports fan's Shangri-la. Every conceivable basketball-related entertainment option was there, most of which had a good view of the court. Restaurants abounded, and there were numerous concession stands, big-screen televisions on every wall, life-size cutouts of the players, and more souvenir shops—the amenities seemed endless. As a huge basketball fan, I thought I was in heaven.

Then something strange happened. I thought the tour was over. I could not imagine how there could be anything else. But our guide said, "Let's get back on the elevator. We have one more stop." *One more stop. What in the world was that going to be?*

How could anything be grander than what I had just seen? I was wrong. There *was* more.

Up one more floor, the elevator doors opened and we arrived on the luxury suites level. Since that's not an area I would normally frequent, I had forgotten about it. Circling the entire arena, these suites had every amenity and convenience you could think of, and you never had to leave your seat or your suite to have them. The game was always in full view, and you had a kitchen, buffet food service, waiters and waitresses, special access to food options not available to the rest of the crowd, big-screen HD televisions—I was overwhelmed. Soon our tour guide informed us that not only did suite owners have access to the suites during games, but they also could use the suite for *any event* that came to the Amway—concerts, the circus, arena football, indoor soccer—you name it! I had definitely been wrong. There was *so much* more.

When it comes to understanding heaven, I think many Christians take the same approach I did before I got to the luxury suites. Mainly due to ignorance or lack of Bible study, we don't understand the last stop. We figuratively get out of the elevator in heaven, and it *is* marvelous. We read the Scriptures that describe it, and it's mind-blowing. It's hard for us to imagine there's anything more, but there is. The voice of God gently reminds us there's one more stop. As immortal beings, heaven is not the final destination. There's more in the new heaven and the new earth, and that's what I want to explore with you in this last chapter.

To be clear, we have an abundance of complex issues related to eschatology—our theology of the endtimes. You'll find a myriad of opinions on the rapture, the millennium, and the tribulation, each with their own substantive and worthwhile arguments. Even so, I do not think God's plan can be completely known. You can spend hours and hours in debate on these topics, but the bottom line is that no one knows for sure. John writes in Revelation 10:4, "And when the seven thunders spoke, I was about to write; but I heard a voice from heaven say, 'Seal up what the seven thunders have said and do not write it down.'" Plain and simple, God has not told us everything. It is laughable to think that we, as finite human beings, can somehow discern the infinite God's exact final plan. If you find someone who says they can, run—fast!

I'm not saying that studying the endtimes isn't valuable. Clearly, much has been revealed to encourage us. I am only saying that exploring such study is not my purpose here. Instead, I want to give you a glimpse of what Scripture reveals about the new heaven and the new earth—the restoration and redemption of all things—and what will be our final dwelling place with God.

A Scriptural Review

Let's consider the four places in Scripture where the new heaven and the new earth are mentioned as God's final plan:

> "See, I will create new heavens and a new earth. The former things will not be remembered, nor will they come to mind. But be glad and rejoice forever in what I will create, for I will create Jerusalem to be a delight and its people a joy. . . . The sound of weeping and of crying will be heard in it no more. . . . Never again will there be in it an infant who lives but a few days, or an old man who does not live out his years. . . . The wolf and the lamb will feed together, and the lion will eat straw like the ox, and dust will be the serpent's food. They will neither harm nor destroy on all my holy mountain," says the Lord.
>
> Isaiah 65:17–20, 25

> "As the new heavens and the new earth that I make will endure before me," declares the Lord, "so will your name and descendants endure. From one New Moon to another and from one Sabbath to another, all mankind will come and bow down before me," says the Lord.
>
> Isaiah 66:22–23

> But in keeping with his promise we are looking forward to a new heaven and a new earth, where righteousness dwells.
>
> 2 Peter 3:13

> Then I saw "a new heaven and a new earth," for the first heaven and the first earth had passed away, and there was no longer any

sea. I saw the Holy City, the New Jerusalem, coming down out of heaven from God, prepared as a bride beautifully dressed for her husband. And I heard a loud voice from the throne saying, "Look! God's dwelling place is now among the people, and he will dwell with them. They will be his people, and God himself will be with them and be their God."

Revelation 21:1–3 (see also vv. 4–5)

In reading these texts, it's important to note that the coming existence of a new heaven and a new earth does not in any way diminish heaven prior to that. Up to the ultimate end of all things, heaven is the dwelling place of God, and those who die in Christ will live in the fullness of his being. After the new heaven and the new earth are brought forth, God comes down to dwell with his people, and again, God's people will live in the fullness of his glorious presence. We need not fear that what we know of heaven will suddenly change in the new heaven and the new earth. It may take on a different form, but the foundation remains the same: we will dwell in the full presence of the almighty God. We will simply be part of God's final plan as it unfolds eternally. Our final dwelling place will be on the renewed and restored earth, the place where heaven and earth come together as God ultimately intended.

In studying these texts, notice the common thread running through them all, which should create a great sense of anticipation in us. Anne Graham Lotz, in her lecture at the Christian Life Conference in 2000,[1] referred to it as the "end of separation." When Revelation 21:1 mentions there will no longer be any sea, it points us to this truth. When you think about it, the sea often separates nation from nation, continent from continent, and people from people. When the sea disappears, all things come together. It is a picture of oneness, unity, wholeness—perfect peace.

In their study of the church in the twenty-first century and the nature of her mission, Kevin DeYoung and Greg Gilbert describe this as the principle of *shalom*. While *shalom* is mentioned often in Scripture, in specific instances it refers to a completed, eternal moment. When *shalom* is used in this way, "It always refers to the new heavens and the new earth. . . . It's true that we enjoy shalom with God now, being justified by faith through Jesus Christ, but the full consummation of that peace will take place only on the last day."[2] Again, we are pointed to a spiritual state of unity, oneness, and peace.

Consider each of the four texts:

Isaiah 65: Lions and lambs feed together. No one is ever hurt. The enmity between God and man is over.

Isaiah 66: All flesh comes to worship the Lord rightly and completely. All are gathered before him as one—shalom to its fullest extent.

2 Peter 3:13: Righteousness dwells there. All conform to God and his standards. No division exists.

Revelation 21: Suffering and evil are gone, and God comes to the new earth to dwell with man. All is reconciled. All relationships are healed. All have become one in and through Christ. It is the manifestation of shalom.[3]

That thread runs through all the images given us in God's Word, and that concept alone should create in us both peace and joyous anticipation of what is eventually to come.

The Importance of the New Heaven and New Earth

Our understanding of this truth is vitally important because it illuminates a core element of God's nature and character. If God only intended to take us to heaven in spiritual form at the moment of our death, then I don't think we'd have these Scripture references—yet we do. They point us to the completed work of God's redemption. God does not discard the world he made; he redeems it. This has always been God's pattern of ultimate grace and love.

When humans fell into sin and became separated from God, we tend to forget that all creation fell too. God cursed the earth when he punished Adam and Eve for their disobedience (Gen. 3:17–19).

So part of God's eternal plan is not simply to redeem our life but to redeem the earth as well. He plans to restore the earth to its original purity and the beauty he created. Referring to Genesis 3, Revelation 22:3 declares, "No longer will there be any curse." When the new earth comes, the triumphant Christ removes the curse he initially imparted and all that went with it. It's why we so enthusiastically sing these words every Christmas:

> No more let sins and sorrows grow,
> Nor thorns infest the ground;
> He comes to make His blessings flow
> Far as the curse is found.[4]

Joy will come to the world because God's original plan for what he made will come to pass. In the original plan, God created the earth to be the physical dwelling place for his creatures, a place where God also came to dwell with Adam and Eve. As we know from God's nature, he will not abandon that plan or what he has made. Author Randy Alcorn writes:

> God has never given up on his original creation. Yet somehow we've managed to overlook an entire biblical vocabulary that makes this point clear. *Reconcile. Redeem. Restore. Recover. Return. Renew. Regenerate. Resurrect.* Each of these biblical words begins with the re- prefix, suggesting a return to an original condition that was ruined or lost. . . . God always sees us in light of what he intended us to be, and he always seeks to restore us to that design.[5]

For a long time in my personal journey, I thought God was going to redeem me by taking me out of this darkened, evil world and whisk me away to a new, spiritual heaven where I would live out my eternity. Instead, with the study of these texts, I realized that he actually intends to redeem the original plan. He will take the earth back to its original form where we, in our resurrected and restored bodies, will dwell.

I have a friend in the car business, and one of his favorite hobbies is to restore classic cars, mainly Ford Mustangs. He can certainly afford to buy a brand-new Mustang and enjoy it, but for him, there is something uniquely special about taking the time and effort to completely restore a car to its original pristine condition. It's almost like going back in time. The old has become new again.

And that is the hope of the gospel. The earth is not merely done away with in favor of something new, nor are we. Instead, God takes our old, worn-out, sinful selves and restores them. He makes us new again, and he will do the same thing with the earth. God does not throw out the old one. He restores it to its original pristine condition.

Therefore, in many respects you *do know* something about your ultimate dwelling place. You will live in immortality on the earth, but it will be the earth in the fullness of God's original plan. It's hard to wrap our human brains around an idea like this, but reflecting on it adds to our hope for the world to come. Peter preached in Acts 3:21, "Heaven must receive him [Jesus] until the time comes for God to restore everything, as he promised long ago through his holy prophets." When we die, there is no doubt we go to heaven, but we still have one more stop to make: the new earth where God restores all things. Restoration and redemption are part of who God is, and we should expect nothing less for the world he made.

Physical Bodily Resurrection

The earth's restoration is great news, but from a personal standpoint, the restoration of the physical body may be even better. Several months ago I started having terrible shooting pains down the left side of my back, up into my shoulder and neck, and then down my left arm. At first I thought I had pulled something, so I did the normal things: rest, ice, and stretching. Nothing helped. I started taking pain relievers and getting physical therapy. Those didn't help. Finally, I called a doctor, who diagnosed me with a herniated disk in my neck. When I got the diagnosis, I was relieved but also frustrated. I suppose when you are fifty years old, these sorts of things start happening. But I told my wife, "This is nuts. With all my other aches and pains, I'm ready to trade this body in on a new model."

I know we all feel that way at times. We are acutely aware of what Paul means in 2 Corinthians 4:16 when he writes, "Outwardly we are wasting away." Our bodies are physical, and eventually they fail. Over time the failures become more evident, and we reminisce about our younger days when our muscles were more supple and our limbs more flexible. That's one of the great things we have to look forward to about the conclusion of God's ultimate plan. We will be raised in bodily, physical form. Paul gives a hint of this in 2 Corinthians 5:1: "For we know that if the earthly tent we live in is destroyed, we have a building from God, an eternal house in heaven, not built by human hands."

More than just the glorified spiritual bodies we experience at the moment of our death, we believe that when Christ returns, those who are in Christ will be physically raised. Paul writes in 1 Corinthians 15:52, "In a flash, in the twinkling of an eye, at the last trumpet. For the trumpet will sound, the dead will be raised imperishable." Paul also writes in 1 Thessalonians 4:16–17:

> The Lord himself will come down from heaven, with a loud command, with the voice of the archangel and with the trumpet call of God, and the dead in Christ will rise first. After that, we who are still alive and are left will be caught up together with them in the clouds to meet the Lord in the air. And so we will be with the Lord forever.

Paul is referring to the moment when we, like Christ, will be physically raised. It will be our old bodies, but they will no longer be the weak, diseased, sin-filled vessels we inhabited initially. No, these will be restored and redeemed, ready for eternity. I know some people get hung up here because they think, *What if I get cremated? I won't have a body to raise.* Remember, part of the curse in Genesis 3 is, "To dust you will return" (v. 19). Whether you're buried or cremated, your body becomes dust; the only question is how fast you get there. But God, in his creative power, redeems and restores our physical bodies at the last day. We were created from dust in the beginning, and God will restore us from dust again in the fulfillment of his eternal plan.

171

Further, we need not fear a missing body part or other physical malady. For example, a pastoral colleague did a funeral for someone who had been killed in a violent car accident. The man's foot had been severed from his body, and authorities did not locate it until some months later, well after the burial. Still, in a somewhat odd request, the family was insistent that the foot be interred with the rest of the body so that he would "have it on the last day." My friend had never done a service for a foot before, and I haven't done once since, but I do know this: God is our Creator, and he is fully capable of restoring our bodies to their original form and redeeming them for eternity. We don't have to bring everything with us.

I'm sure you have other questions, most of which I doubt I can answer. I don't know if we'll eat or if we'll wear clothes or what age we will be or many other details like that. I do know, however, that we will never again contend with pain or injury or disease. As I said before, there will be no more herniated discs or arthritis or cancer or lupus. All those things go away. The great Welsh preacher Martyn Lloyd-Jones wrote:

> Everything will be glorified, even nature itself. And that seems to me to be the biblical teaching about the eternal state: that what we call heaven is life in this perfect world as God intended humanity to live it. When he put Adam in paradise at the beginning, Adam fell, and all fell with him, but men and women are meant to live in the body, and will live in a glorified body in a glorified world, and God will be with them.[6]

On the last day we will receive new, restored physical bodies. And they never break. And they never hurt. I'm really looking forward to that.

God Will Make His Dwelling with Us

As I said in the previous chapter, heaven is the dwelling place of God. It is the place where we will eternally exist in the fullness of all that he is. And when the new heaven and new earth are brought down, they become his dwelling place. Throughout the Old Testament, God's Word foretells his future glory on earth.

> For the LORD will rebuild Zion and appear in his glory.
>
> Psalm 102:16

> In a little while I will once more shake the heavens and the earth, the sea and the dry land. I will shake all nations, and what is desired by all nations will come, and I will fill this house with glory.
>
> Haggai 2:6–7

> I saw the glory of the God of Israel coming from the east . . . and the land was radiant with his glory.
>
> Ezekiel 43:2

In each instance and many others, the Old Testament points to a future time when the earth will be redeemed and the glory and presence of the Lord will be found therein. In no way is the earth to be destroyed or done away with, but rather it will be renewed in such a way that the glorious presence of God will come to dwell.

In fact, that has been God's manner from the beginning of creation. In the perfection of Eden, God walked in the garden with Adam and Eve. The creatures he made did not dwell with him in heaven; God came down to dwell with them. Even before sin entered in, God came to dwell with us. In the misery and darkness of our sin, God came down again in Christ to save us. Christianity is the only religious tradition in the world that makes such a declaration. God comes down. Every other tradition holds that humankind must do something to move up—to merit an eternity in heaven.

God's constant movement toward us, to be present with us, has its fullest expression in his final plan. On the last day, when he brings all things under submission to his glory, John declares: "I heard a loud voice from the throne saying, 'Look! God's dwelling place is now among the people, and he will dwell with them'" (Rev. 21:3).

Jesus made a similar promise: "Anyone who loves me will obey my teaching. My Father will love them, and we will come to them and make our home with them" (John 14:23). Clearly, that can be interpreted to mean God's presence in the earthly life of the believer, but it is also a statement of truth. God always moves toward us. He always comes to live with us, and that will continue to be true in the end.

On that last day, his dwelling is with us and that dwelling is the New Jerusalem. The new earth and the new heaven come down together from God—a beyond-this-world merger that defies human comprehension. The new earth becomes God's "Holy City" (Rev. 21:2), and again, God comes to us. Even as the Christ child was called Immanuel (which means "God with us"), so God remains true to that name. In the end, he lives with us on the restored earth where all will gather before him in worship.

A Work Solely Belonging to God

Even with these wonderful truths, we need to take notice of a recent wave of new scholarship that has proven problematic, and ultimately confusing, when considering this subject. Journalist Jon Meacham summed up the breadth of these positions in an article for *Time* magazine, asking the question, "What if Christianity is not about enduring this sinful, fallen world in search of a reward and eternal rest? What if God brings together heaven and earth in a wholly new, wholly redeemed creation?"[7]

Meacham summarizes the conflicts currently created: Is heaven the spiritual place where we go to find rest and peace from the perils of this life, or is heaven actually the restoration of the earth that ultimately becomes God's dwelling place? In the world of theological scholarship, it appears that those who discuss heaven as an idyllic paradise of peace and rest must be pitted against those who see it as the coming restoration of the earth and the New Jerusalem. I disagree with that premise. It's not an either-or proposition. It's both-and.

1. Heaven *is* the spiritual home for those who die in Christ, but it *is not* a boring place where we sit with winged cherubs playing harps all day. That kind of greeting-card, oversimplified

view of the spiritual heaven drains it of its glorious meaning. We've already looked at Scripture that shows us we are
immediately taken by Jesus to be with God where he is—in
heaven. That is a current, wondrous, and yet humanly incon-
ceivable spiritual reality. We won't fully understand it until
we get there, but based on what we know about the nature
of God, we can be assured of its wonder.

2. It is also true that when God brings his final plan to completion on the last day, heaven and earth will merge into one—a
   place where we live in resurrected physical bodies in the
   presence of the living, almighty God.

In his article, Meacham suggests that in today's world, the pearly
gates view of heaven and the new earth view of heaven must op-
pose each other. To the contrary, trying to separate these two truths
diminishes the testimony of the biblical witness on both of these
realities while creating a challenging issue for how we live in the
present.

Separating them into opposites suggests we must take one of
two approaches: (1) we dismiss this current world and its evils in
favor of reflecting on the heaven that is to come, or (2) we invest
in this world because we recognize that it will one day be restored.
I don't think we have to make that choice. I believe we do both.
Clearly, the earth matters to God. Scholars such as N. T. Wright
and Christopher Morse suggest that the coming *new earth* means
we must work harder for the earth's restoration. Meacham writes:

> This point of view is one in which the alleviation of the evident pain
> and injustice of the world is the ongoing work that Jesus began and
> the means of bringing into being what the New Testament authors
> meant when they spoke of heaven. . . . One should neither need nor
> want a ticket out of the created order into an ethereal realm. One
> should instead be hard at work making the world godly and just.[8]

In other words, if we think this planet will be destroyed in the
end while we live in heaven for eternity, then we likely won't care
much about this place while we're here. If, on the other hand, we

believe that this world is not destroyed in the end but that we will ultimately live on earth in a redeemed fashion, then we will be more committed to the stewardship of it. That is an unfortunate dichotomy. Why shouldn't we be doing that anyway? This is the earth God gave us. Of course we should seek its restoration. Of course we should faithfully serve to make this world more godly and just. I believe in *creation care*. We are all called as faithful stewards of what God has made. We must always be about the task he gave us in Genesis to rule over the earth and subdue it (Gen. 1:28). That is a command to not abuse the earth but to honor God by how we use the resources of this planet. It can never be one or the other. It's both.

On the other hand, we cannot diminish our promised heavenly reward by thinking of it as just a doctrine that provides hope and strength in our current sufferings. Our central Florida community saw this firsthand recently in the racially charged killing of Trayvon Martin, a young black male, by local neighborhood watch volunteer George Zimmerman. In a CNN interview, Trayvon's mother said, "I believe Trayvon is in heaven with God, and he has on a hoodie." Was it wrong for her to find solace in her grief by looking to the peace and justice of heaven? Of course not. She was declaring what so many believe: heaven is a relief from this world's pain and peril. But it's not *only* that. There's more, and that's the Good News of the gospel. We do not set the new earth as something *opposed* to the promise of heaven, but as the biblical truth that *completes* the promise of heaven.

We also need to further understand our role and responsibility in how the new earth is formed. It is not *ours* to bring or create. It is not our responsibility to assume. We cannot elevate the value of our works by falsely assuming our care of the earth will speed its ultimate transformation. That type of works-oriented view will crush us. If I believe I can ultimately contribute to the full restoration of this earth, I will be enormously disappointed. It's Sisyphus pushing the rock up the hill. It's not a sustainable life because there's no hope in it. It cannot be done. Because of the sin that fills our hearts and darkens our world, no amount of human effort will ever bring restoration to the earth. That has always been the sole work of God.

The earth's ultimate redemption can only happen when Christ returns, and that is where we place our hope. I serve Christ in this world because I know the promise of what is to come *and* because those who dwell here need God's love and grace. My understanding of what heaven will be like *and* my knowledge of the full redemption of the earth serve as the ground for my hope and faith. The combination of those two things creates the full message of God's truth—the truth that all Christians should proclaim. As one of my seminary professors used to say, "Babylon will always be Babylon." As long as sinful people fill the earth, it will always be less than God's original design and plan.

Does that mean we cannot effect some change in it now? Of course not. We seek the kingdom of God now. Through Christ, the kingdom of God has been brought near to us (Luke 10:9). We see it and experience it by his Holy Spirit. Thus we work, often through the ministry of the church, to usher in that kingdom, but we do so in the knowledge that it will never be fully completed until God does his ultimate work. If I minister now believing that such kingdom work is mine, then I'll become exhausted and give up. If I take on the responsibility of bringing God's kingdom in some way, then I'll be crushed by that weight. But if I minister and serve knowing that my task is to offer Christ's hope and grace to others even as I look forward to God's coming work, then I am energized. It's God's work and not mine. He will bring it to fruition, and its coming in no way depends on me.

For example, in Revelation 21:5 God announces from his throne, "I am making everything new!" Hebrews 11:10 says that Abraham "was looking forward to the city with foundations, whose architect and builder is God." God creates it, redeems it, and gives it. It is God's work, and thus we eagerly minister and serve him in anticipation of what is to come. Kevin DeYoung and Greg Gilbert write:

> When eternity finally comes, we will live in a land that was made and created *for us*, under a kingdom that was won and established

for us by a Savior who died and was resurrected *for us*. Put simply, the gospel is the Good News of salvation, in all its parts, that is *for us*, and not in the least *by us*.[9]

Similar Yet Different

Naturally, when we hear that the earth and all that is in it will be restored, our minds start to wander down the road toward, *What does that mean? What will it look like? Will we still play baseball? Will the Cubs win the World Series? Will bacon be good for you?* I get that. Trust me, my mind goes there too. Unfortunately, I do not believe there are definitive answers to those questions other than the ones we have discussed. I do know that we will be one unified, redeemed people living forever in the presence of the living God. Thus, whatever we will be doing will be beyond even our wildest imaginations.

That said, I think we are able to deduce two things. First, the new earth will be radically and wholly different from the old one. Scripture repeatedly tells us about the perils of the earth, the dominion where the prince of darkness still reigns. The earth is a fallen, cursed place, and as we think about our future, none of us want any part of living here forever. Thankfully, God promises us that all those things go away. The enemy is defeated. Tears and mourning and pain and suffering all disappear. You get the picture. The new earth will be *very different* from the old one.

At the same time, however, the new earth will be uniquely similar to the old one. Paul writes in Romans 8:20–21:

> For the creation was subjected to frustration, not by its own choice, but by the will of the one who subjected it, in hope that the creation itself will be liberated from its bondage to decay and brought into the freedom and glory of the children of God.

Paul is specifically addressing what ultimately happens to what God created—the earth. Psalm 19:1 proclaims, "The heavens *declare the glory of God*; and the firmament shows His handiwork" (NKJV,

178

italics mine). What God has made declares his glory, but in this fallen world, it has been unable to do so fully.

When the new earth comes, this same creation will fully declare God's glory. It's the same creation, but it will be living out its purpose fully. You will recognize the created order, but it will function in a way previously unseen. Charles Spurgeon offers a helpful image. As Kevin DeYoung and Greg Gilbert describe it, he envisions

> a vast orchestra, poised with their bows drawn, their mallets raised, their fingers on the cello and violin strings, their mouths open as if ready to sing—and yet totally still, covered with cobwebs, and unable to accomplish the task for which they were gathered. The problem? The conductor has defaulted; he, like mankind, has failed to step to the dais to direct the symphony of creation, and so now creation waits, both in frustration and in eager expectation, for the conductor to arrive and begin the music. On the last day, when the sons of God are revealed . . . they will finally follow the Lord to the dais. The bows will move, the mallets will fall, the voices will rise, and the music will begin. The creation will be released from its bondage and restored to its original purpose—the unfettered and unfrustrated praise of God.[10]

It is the same creation. In many respects it will look familiar. But it will be set free to engage with God and for God in a way we have never known. What a beautiful image Spurgeon gives us.

Without question, these are complex and challenging concepts to try to understand and internalize as part of our faith. As I said at the start, it is somewhat laughable for us to even think we can grasp all that God has planned for us and for this world at the end. Therefore, I think it best to conclude with the simplicity of a children's story. Often the most complex issues can be uncovered when described in their simplest form, and in our heart of hearts, we are all *children* of the living God.

C. S. Lewis was one of the most influential Christian writers and thinkers of the last century, but his greatest contribution may well be his series of children's stories called the Chronicles of Narnia. To say they are merely children's stories does them an injustice since they contain some of the most beautiful presentations of the gospel ever written. Some of these stories were made into big-screen movies that bring life to the great adventures and great battles, all centered on four children who move back and forth between this world and the magical land of Narnia. Good battles evil. Danger lurks. Courage rises. Children become warriors. Lessons are learned. And through it all, the central figure is Aslan, the Great Lion—whom many uphold as the Christ figure.

In many respects, the seventh and final book in the series, *The Last Battle*, mirrors what we have talked about in this chapter. It is the end of all things and a discussion of what happens when the end comes. Narnia, the great land created by Aslan, is destroyed. The children deeply mourn the loss even though they continue to journey with Aslan toward his country, or heaven. What transpires at that moment reflects the biblical revelation of the new earth. Randy Alcorn recounts this in *Heaven*, and it is well worth including here:

> "Those hills," said Lucy, "the nice woody ones and the blue ones behind—aren't they very like the southern border of Narnia?"
>
> "Like!" cried Edmund after a moment's silence. "Why they're exactly like. Look, there's Mount Pire with his forked head, and there's the pass into Archenland and everything!"
>
> "And yet they're not like," said Lucy. "They're different. They have more colours on them and they look further away than I remembered and they're more . . . more . . . oh, I don't know. . . ."
>
> "More like the real thing," said the Lord Digory softly.
>
> Suddenly Farsight the Eagle spread his wings, soared thirty or forty feet up into the air, circled round and then alighted on the ground.
>
> "Kings and Queens," he cried, "we have all been blind. We are only beginning to see where we are. From up there I have seen it all—Ettinsmuir, Beaversdam, the Great River, and Cair Paravel still shining on the edge of the Eastern Sea. Narnia is not dead. This is Narnia."
>
> "But how can it be?" said Peter. "For Aslan told us older ones that we should never return to Narnia, and here we are."
>
> "Yes," said Eustace. "And we saw it all destroyed and the sun put out."

"And it's all so different," said Lucy.

"The Eagle is right," said the Lord Digory. "Listen, Peter. When Aslan said you could never go back to Narnia, he meant the Narnia you were thinking of. But that was not the real Narnia. That had a beginning and an end. It was only a shadow or a copy of the real Narnia, which has always been here and always will be here: just as our own world, England and all, is only a shadow or copy of something in Aslan's real world. You need not mourn over Narnia, Lucy. All of the old Narnia that mattered, all the dear creatures, have been drawn into the real Narnia through the Door. And of course it is different; as different as a real thing is from a shadow or as waking life is from a dream. . . ."

The difference between the old Narnia and the new Narnia was like that. The new one was a deeper country: every rock and flower and blade of grass looked as if it meant more. I can't describe it any better than that: if you ever get there, you will know what I mean.

It was the Unicorn who summed up what everyone was feeling. He stamped his right fore-hoof on the ground and neighed and then cried:

"I have come home at last! This is my real country! I belong here. This is the land I have been looking for all my life, though I never knew it till now. The reason why we loved the old Narnia is that it sometimes looked a little like this."[11]

I know I have felt it at times. I have felt that internal nagging, that deep sense that this is not actually my home. I know I was made and meant for something more, and yet I do encounter moments in this life when I taste a bit of what that *something more* is all about:

holding tightly the one you love

staring at the miracle of a newborn baby

standing alongside another as the Holy Spirit opens blind eyes to the love of Christ

taking in all the color and brilliance of a sunrise or sunset

the overwhelming look of gratitude on the face of a prisoner when someone has come to visit the way cold milk and chocolate cake converge as they descend over the tongue

the way it feels to have given all you have in a common cause

the delight of deep, restful sleep

the smell of blooming flowers in spring

the comfort of one hand sliding gently into yours

and even those last moments as a person turns his or her eyes toward God and draws his or her last breath

These are glimpses and foreshadowings of what we know is to come but what we do not yet know.

One day we will dwell on the earth as it was originally created to be. Now we can know it only as a distant and unfulfilled dream. Then we will be home—finally, fully, and eternally home. Then our journey from this life to the next—our journey to everlasting life—will be over, and what a journey it will have been.

May you continue on your journey of faith, your journey in this life, alive and assured of what is to come, filled by the strength and hope that springs from the knowledge that one day you will declare, "I have come home at last!" Praise God.

Notes

Introduction

1. John Cloud, "A Kinder, Gentler Death," *Time*, September 18, 2000.

2. Kirk Johnson, "Town Breathes Easier as Frozen Dead Guy and His Festival Stay Put," *New York Times*, January 3, 2012.

3. Simon Critchley, *The Book of Dead Philosophers* (New York: Vintage, 2008), 247.

4. Anna Quindlen, "Public and Private: Life after Death," *New York Times*, May 4, 1994.

5. Emily Dickinson, "The Last Night That She Lived," *The Complete Poems of Emily Dickinson*, ed. Thomas H. Johnson (New York: Little, Brown, 1960), 497.

6. For a full treatment on this subject, see my book *Learning to Be You: How Our True Identity in Christ Sets Us Free* (Grand Rapids: Baker, 2012).

7. The History Place Great Speeches Collection, www.historyplace.com/speeches/rfk-mlk.htm.

8. John Donne, "Death Be Not Proud," Herbert J. C. Grierson, *Metaphysical Lyrics and Poems of the 17th Century* (Oxford: Clarendon Press, 1921), 244; http://www.bartleby.com/105/72.html.

9. Billy Graham, *Nearing Home: Life, Faith, and Finishing Well* (Nashville: Thomas Nelson, 2011).

10. Dietrich Bonhoeffer, "No One Has Yet Believed," *Dietrich Bonhoeffer Works*, vol. 13, London: 1933–35, ed. Keith Clements, trans. Isabel Best (Minneapolis: Fortress, 2007), 331.

Chapter 1: What's Going On Here?

1. C. S. Lewis, "The Weight of Glory," sermon, Church of St. Mary the Virgin, Oxford, England, June 8, 1941. Published in *Theology*, November 1941.

2. Gordon Fee, *New International Commentary on the New Testament: The First Epistle to the Corinthians* (Grand Rapids: Eerdmans, 1987), 797.

3. While the predictions and descriptions of Revelation are complex, my purpose is not to examine or explain them here.

4. Ellen Goodman, "Nothing is Forever," *Boston Globe*, August 9, 2008.

Chapter 2: How Do I Handle It?

1. David Powers, "Japan: No Surrender in World War II," February 17, 2011, http://www.bbc.co.uk/history/worldwars/wwtwo/japan_no_surrender_01.shtml.

2. W. D. C. Wagiswara, *The Buddha's Way of Virtue* (New York: Evinity Publishing, 2009), 26.

3. C. S. Lewis, *The Last Battle* (New York: Macmillan, 1956), 184.

Chapter 3: What Do I Say? What Do I Do?

1. Elisabeth Kübler-Ross, *On Death and Dying* (New York: Macmillan, 1969).

2. Charmaine Griffiths, quoted in "How Hugs Can Aid Women's Hearts," BBC News, August 8, 2005, www.bbc.co.uk/2/hi/4131508.stm.

3. William Wordsworth, "Ode: Intimations of Immortality from Recollection of Early Childhood," *The Oxford Book of English Verse*, ed. Arthur Quiller-Couch (Oxford: Clarendon, 1919), 536.

Chapter 4: How Do I Live with Loss?

1. Tim Hansel, *You Gotta Keep Dancin'* (Elgin, IL: David C. Cook, 1985), 15.

2. John G. Stackhouse Jr., "Harleys in Heaven," *Christianity Today*, June 2003, 38.

3. T. E. Holt, MD, "What We Learn from the Dying," *Men's Health*, November 2007, 190.

4. Anna Quindlen, *Every Last One* (New York: Random House, 2010), 199.

5. Joyce Carol Oates, *A Widow's Story* (New York: HarperCollins, 2011), 408.

6. Henry van Dyke, "Gone from My Sight," http://thinkexist.com/quotation/i-am-standing-upon-the-seashore-a-ship-at-my-side/1273248.html.

Chapter 5: How Will We Find Our Way Home?

1. C. S. Lewis, *Mere Christianity* (New York: Macmillan, 1952), 120.

2. Dante, *The Inferno*, canto 1, lines 1–7.

3. John Bunyan, *Pilgrim's Progress*, available online at http://www.ccel.org/ccel/bunyan/pilgrim/html.

4. J. Ramsey Michaels, *The Gospel of John*, New International Commentary on the New Testament (Grand Rapids: Eerdmans, 2010), 766.

5. George Beasley-Murray, *John*, Word Biblical Commentary (Waco: Word, 1987), 248–49.

6. Craig Barnes, *Searching for Home* (Grand Rapids: Brazos, 2003), 147.

7. Michaels, *Gospel of John*, 769.

Notes

Chapter 6: Why Not Go to Heaven Now?

1. See "Jury Awards Nearly $3 Million to Portland-Area Couple in 'Wrongful Birth' Lawsuit against Legacy Health," by Aimee Green, *The Oregonian*, March 9, 2012, http://www.oregonlive.com/portland/index.ssf/2012/03/jury_rules_in _portland-area_co.html.

2. Fred Hutchison, "Postmodernism," *Renew America*, March 22, 2012, www.renewamerica.com.

3. Woody Allen, interview in *Esquire*, March 1977, 64.

4. Michael Wines, "Bystanders' Neglect of Injured Toddler Sets Off Soul-Searching on Web Sites in China," *New York Times*, October 19, 2011, A9.

5. Cyril C. Richardson, ed., *Early Christian Fathers* (New York: Simon and Schuster, 1996), 175. From the primary document "The So-Called Letter to Diognetus: The Mystery of the New People."

6. Quoted in Rodney Stark, *The Rise of Christianity* (New York: HarperOne, 1996), 76.

7. *The Westminster Confession of Faith and Larger Catechism* (Philadelphia: Presbyterian and Reformed, 2011), 59.

8. Fyodor Dostoevsky, *The Brothers Karamazov* (New York: Modern Library, 1996), 756, italics mine.

9. Quoted in Mary Bosanquet, *The Life and Death of Dietrich Bonhoeffer* (New York: Harper & Row, 1969), 109.

Chapter 7: What Is Heaven Like?

1. Billy Graham, "Life Forever with Jesus," *Decision*, August 1, 2007, 38.

2. "The Evangelistic Question That Died," *Christianity Today*, March 12, 2012, 9.

3. Critchley, *Book of Dead Philosophers*, 247; Jon Meacham, "Heaven Can't Wait," *Time*, April 16, 2012, 32.

4. Anne Graham Lotz, "Heaven," lecture at Christian Life Conference, Montreat Conference Center, Montreat, NC, July 3, 2000.

5. Jane Kenyon, "Notes from the Other Side," in *Constance* (St. Paul, MN: Graywolf Press, 1993).

6. Forrest McCann, *Hymns and History: An Annotated Survey of Sources* (Abilene, TX: ACU Press, 1997).

7. Venerable Bede, a sermon preached on All Saint's Day ca. 710, quoted in William Jennings Bryan, ed., *The World's Famous Quotations* (New York: Funk and Wagnalls, 1906).

8. Randy Alcorn, *Heaven* (Wheaton: Tyndale, 2004), 328.

9. Julie Gold, "Heaven," from *Dream Loud*, Gadfly Records, 1998.

10. George Matheson, "O Love That Wilt Not Let Me Go," *Church of Scotland*, January 1882.

11. *The Westminster Standards* (Suwanee, GA: Great Commission Publications, 2011), 32.

12. Victor Frankl, *Man's Search for Meaning* (New York: Pocket Books, 1997), 25.

13. Fran Walsh, Philippa Boyens, Peter Jackson, *The Lord of the Rings: The Return of the King*, 2003, Box Office Films, http://www.imsdb.com/scripts/Lord-of-the-Rings-Return-of-the-King.html, accessed December 11, 2009.

Chapter 8: What Happens in the End?

1. Anne Graham Lotz, "Heaven."
2. Kevin DeYoung and Greg Gilbert, *What Is the Mission of the Church?* (Wheaton: Crossway, 2011), 203.
3. Ibid., 204.
4. Isaac Watts, "Joy to the World," 1719.
5. Alcorn, *Heaven*, 88.
6. Martyn Lloyd-Jones, quoted in ibid., 99.
7. John Meacham, "Heaven Can't Wait," *Time*, April 16, 2012, 34.
8. Ibid.
9. DeYoung and Gilbert, *What Is the Mission of the Church?*, 208, emphasis added.
10. Ibid., 216.
11. Lewis, *Last Battle*, 168–71.

David D. Swanson is senior pastor of the 4,000-member First Presbyterian Church of Orlando. He is also the cofounder and principal teacher for The Well, a national media ministry featured on the Trinity Broadcasting Network and online at www.drink fromthewell.com. He is the author of *Learning to Be You*, *Vital Signs*, and *The Essentials*. He lives in Florida with his wife and has three college-aged children.

How Your True Identity
Sets You Free

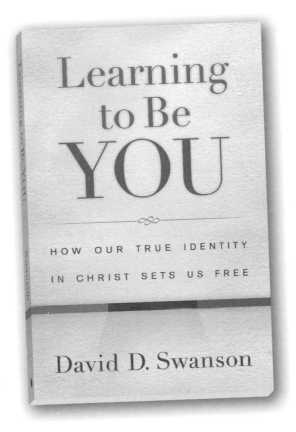

"By reading this book you will find your own soul encouraged and your life infused with purpose and direction. David has most certainly captured the reality of what it means when a person understands that 'God loves you and has a wonderful plan for your life!'"

—Vonette Bright, cofounder, Campus Crusade for Christ/Cru

Hear David Swanson on TBN's *The Well*

David Swanson shares a weekly message presenting biblical truths that are real and relevant, airing on TBN and The Church Channel.

Check http://www.tbn.org/watch-us/broadcast-schedule for times in your area or watch online at www.drinkfromthewell.com.